WILLIAM TEMPLE

A Calling to Prophecy

To the memory of

Peter Hinchliff

1929–1995

WILLIAM TEMPLE

A Calling to Prophecy

Stephen Spencer

Published in Great Britain in 2001 by SPCK
Holy Trinity Church
Marylebone Road
London NW1 4DU

British Library Cataloguing-in-Publication Data
A catalogue record for this book is available from the British Library.

ISBN 0-281-05437-1

Typeset by Kenneth Burnley, Wirral, Cheshire.
Printed in Great Britain by
The Cromwell Press, Trowbridge, Wiltshire.

Contents

Foreword

Archbishop William Temple was undoubtedly one of the great men of the twentieth century. The issues with which he concerned himself – social welfare for all, education, ecumenism and evangelism – remain at the heart of the Church's life today. William Temple had immense gifts and, not least, the ability to overcome the barriers of class, Christian denomination and political allegiance. He was recognized as both a man of God and a man of the people. Most of those who met him were inspired by the encounter.

In this new study of Temple's life, published to coincide with the celebration of the seventy-fifth anniversary of his foundation of the diocese of Blackburn, Stephen Spencer captures Temple's religious and intellectual pilgrimage and describes the significant contribution which he made to the life of the Church and the nation in the first half of the twentieth century. The author rightly comes to the conclusion that William Temple was 'a prophet, albeit a rather reasonable, jovial and consensus-seeking one'. One might be tempted to say that he was the kind of prophet the Church of England at its best should produce!

Some believe that the contemporary Church lacks its prophets. They may be right, but this book proves that William Temple's prophecy rested on an ability to use his considerable intellectual gifts, his faith in the incarnate Lord, and the opportunities life offered to him, to engage in mission for Christ. In doing this he helped to bring hope and new opportunities to the lives of millions.

I am most grateful to Stephen Spencer for giving us the opportunity to reconsider the contribution William Temple made. I commend the book to all who wish seriously to engage with the interface between the gospel, the Church and life today.

+ ALAN BLACKBURN

Preface

William Temple was born, as they say, of the purple. While history might not yet record him as such, his father was at least William's equal. Unlike William, however, Frederick had to make his own way from the most restricted of circumstances to the throne of St Augustine, then a social pinnacle in the British Empire, and a position therefore of some very significant political influence. Frederick Temple, at long last, has gained a biographer to match his importance with Peter Hinchliff's *Frederick Temple* (1998). Unlike William, too, Frederick was direct to the point of being rude. To a half-witted clergyman requesting non-residence in his parish on the grounds that his house was only three miles away as the crow flies, Frederick replied that the priest was no crow. Non-residency was refused.

While William's start at work could not have been more different from his father's, in inheriting the advantages of being the son of the Primate of All England, William also acquired the inevitable disadvantages confronting any offspring born to a father who was, if grudgingly, recognized by his peers as a towering success. Moreover, his father's success had been won by sheer ability and owed nothing to the exercise on his own behalf of his undoubted political skills.

Frederick's style was in marked contrast to his oily successor, Randall Davidson. Frederick, while valuing Davidson's abilities, could be abrupt with the latter's ingratiating manner. For example, when Davidson offered a meat lozenge to the near-blind and visibly tottering Archbishop during the crowning of Edward VII, Frederick curtly replied that it was his legs that were giving out, not his throat.

In contrast, as Stephen Spencer makes clear in this fine study, William was a seeker of the 'third way' long before such a phrase began whizzing around the political arena. It was a third way based on a highly developed set of principles. It was also a third way which William relentlessly pursued during most of his 63-year life. Had he been as neurotic as was Mr Gladstone in recording how each day had been spent, the resulting diary pages would have burned with an energy unleashed upon that whole series of events which make up the life of a priest and bishop. At two points in the text here William's ability to work as though he were six people is frighteningly illustrated.

Temple saw Christianity, in part, as a social religion. I say 'in part' because the social dimension grew naturally from his understanding of God and his creation and could not be separated from these most fundamental of beliefs. The social faith was in no way an appendage shoe-horned on to his religious beliefs.

What Stephen Spencer makes so clear (and it is just one area where the book cuts new ground) are the theological roots of Temple's socio-political creed. I have yet to read an explanation of Temple's thinking set out so succinctly or as comprehensively as it appears in this book. Stephen Spencer also makes a judgement about the importance of Temple's political creed in acting as a stimulus to, as well as giving confidence and direction to the best of radical forces during the inter-war years. This is just one aspect of the book which will form the basis of much future debate.

What will also be debated is Stephen Spencer's major theme that Temple was a prophet, albeit a very reasonable one. Was Temple an instrument of God's kingdom? Temple's greatest achievement to me was to instil some of his own confidence into working-class voters, ensuring their resolve against returning after war-time to the life of the 1930s. Yet even to measure Temple in terms of prophecy will be to fire a debate on the links, if any, between building and giving weight to a specific political programme, as Temple did, and the seeking of a kingdom which is already in our midst.

This is, as I say, only one of the many parts of this study which will ignite debate. Here is the best portrait in the round of William Temple, and there can be little question about the abilities the author has brought to the study.

The influence of Christianity has declined apace in the decades since Temple's early death. That someone of Stephen Spencer's abilities is attracted to the priesthood hints that the future for Christianity in Britain is perhaps not as dark as some of us all too often assume. That Stephen Spencer has also been drawn to Temple gives another, more immediate insight into Temple's status and power to win over some of the very best young intellects of a generation, while simultaneously standing alongside those who still await the call to the rich man's table.

FRANK FIELD, MP

Introduction

The cartoon by Low on the front cover, from the London *Evening Standard* of April 1943, identifies William Temple as a figure of huge public significance for English Christianity in the middle years of the twentieth century. Temple, as Archbishop of Canterbury, had just addressed a massed audience at the Albert Hall on the theme of the Church looking forward to the post-Second World War world. He had made some controversial remarks about the moral duties of banks and the terms on which they should lend money. Many from the City of London thought his remarks naïve and criticized him heavily in the press. Others saw his remarks (whatever the merit of their detail) as pointing to the need for real social justice in the forthcoming post-war reconstruction. He sharply divided public opinion but, more importantly, as Low shows, he raised the public profile and moral influence of the Christian gospel. The country was looking forward to post-war reconstruction: Temple represented the 'Christian aim' for that future as he faced down the bulldogs of high finance, and so allowed a Christian vision to carry significant influence.

That he had a lasting influence is confirmed by Edward Heath, in a foreword to the 1976 edition of Temple's own *Christianity and Social Order*. Heath wrote:

> The impact of William Temple on my generation was immense
> . . . The reason was not far to seek. William Temple was
> foremost among the leaders of the nation, temporal or spiritual,

in posing challenging, radical questions about the nature of our society. Most important of all, he propounded with lucidity and vigour his understanding of the Christian ethic in its application to the contemporary problems which engrossed us all.

The year 2001 marks two anniversaries that bring William Temple's name and achievements before the public eye once more. First, it is the seventy-fifth anniversary of Temple's founding of the diocese of Blackburn in the Northern Province of the Church of England, which took place when he was the Bishop of Manchester. It was Temple who set in motion and enthusiastically encouraged the dividing of that diocese, the second largest in England at that time, into two. This created a new diocese in its northern half, an area now coterminous with the county of Lancashire.

2001 also marks the sixtieth anniversary of the Malvern Conference on the life of the Church and the order of society. This was a conference called and chaired by Temple in 1941, a gathering of theologians and church leaders that played a significant role in moving Christian public opinion towards supporting post-war reconstruction and the establishing of the welfare state. The conference led to Temple's writing and publishing *Christianity and Social Order* in 1942, a Penguin special that sold an astonishing 139,000 copies. This, too, left its mark upon political attitudes at the time.

These anniversaries remind us of both Temple's historical importance and also of the increasing distance that now lies between him and us. The number of clergy who knew and worked with him and who are still alive today is very small. The times in which he lived have now passed from our own century into 'the last century'. The theology and philosophy that he lived and breathed can seem very remote from the postmodern world we inhabit.

For both these reasons, that is his importance and his increasing remoteness, the time is right for a new study of Temple. This book presents an outline of his life and thought to those who are unfamiliar with it, and looks at Temple's continuing importance for the life of the churches and society today. It is written for clergy, lay people and students who know little about Temple. The official biography, by F. A. Iremonger, remains the main source of information about his life, and it usefully reprints a large number of his letters. But it is now very dated in its style and approach, and it is too hagiographical to give an adequate assessment of its subject.

There has been the need for some time for a new life of Temple. The 1992 book by John Kent, *William Temple*, a study of Temple's political significance within British society between the two world wars, contains some fresh research into its subject but, by definition, does not give a rounded presentation of his life and thought. The pages that follow, while not amounting to a full-scale biography, do endeavour to tell the story of his life in a positive yet critical way, and within that to include an account of his philosophical, theological and ethical thought. For the first time among the books on Temple they present an outline of his thought within the unfolding story of his life. Finally, they attempt to assess Temple not on the basis of his career as a churchman alone, nor on his philosophical theology alone, but on the basis of the two seen together.

The story begins with Temple's childhood at Fulham Palace, and follows him through his education at Rugby and Oxford to his adult work as a philosophy lecturer, headmaster, rector, campaigner, cathedral canon, theologian, editor, diocesan bishop, Archbishop of York and finally his brief spell as Archbishop of Canterbury. As Temple's career developed, and as he became engaged in a huge range of interests, it is possible to see a unifying thread running through his work. This thread was the presenting of an ideal, in particular the outline of a renewed world he believed God in Christ was bringing about, with the teaching and campaigning work of trying to move people towards its realization. And, as we shall see, when he was a young man he came to believe that he was called, along with others, to be a prophet of the coming of that world. As we follow Temple through the course of his life, the question that naturally arises is this: did he rise to such a calling over the years? Did he actually become a prophet to the Church and the nation? And does he therefore have an enduring prophetic significance for the churches today, as they begin a new century with its very different challenges and opportunities?

*   *   *

I am very grateful to Joan Temple, wife of the late Bishop Frederick Temple, William Temple's nephew, for permission to reprint a number of extracts from William Temple's letters.

*   *   *

This book would not have been completed without the help and encouragement of some good friends. To Alan Charters and his enthusiasm for nineteenth- and twentieth-century religious thought and history I am indebted for my long-standing interest in this area; to Oliver O'Donovan I am indebted for detailed and constructive guidance in my research on Temple; to Stephen Platten I am greatly indebted for detailed corrections and suggestions on the first draft of this book, and for unflagging encouragement over the years. My debt to Adrian Hastings' writings will be apparent at many points in the book; I am also indebted to him for reading and correcting the first draft. To my wife Sally I owe great help with fighting the battles of style and presentation. The errors and oddities of style and content that remain are entirely my own. To Tim Herbert and Bishop Alan Chesters I am indebted for support for this project. Lastly, to Peter Hinchliff I owe the teaching and warm encouragement that allowed me to undertake research in this area in the first place. To his memory these pages are dedicated with gratitude.

Brookhouse
Lancashire

CHAPTER 1

From Palace to Priesthood

Victorian upbringing

William Temple was born on 15 October 1881, into a world very different from our own. The social differences are brilliantly captured in a description of a typical day at Fulham Palace, the official residence of Temple's elderly father, Frederick Temple, who was at that time the Bishop of London. The palace was William's home until the age of 15 (though he had been born in Exeter when his father was bishop there). He had one older brother, Frederick, and, according to F. A. Iremonger,

> The day at Fulham began with prayers in the Palace Chapel. For this there was a well-established ceremonial. The boys waited in the vestry, which was separated from the chapel by a stone-flagged passage. The butler also waited, with the Bishop's surplice over his arm, and passed the time cleaning his finger-nails for the day with a pocket-knife. Mrs Temple and other ladies would come hurrying down the passage, followed by the Bishop. He never stopped, but kissed each of his sons as he walked on; and the butler put his surplice over the Bishop's arms extended backwards, and on to his shoulders. The boys fell in beside their father, who put his arms around them, looking (as was remarked) like a large angel with wings as he entered the chapel. He turned into his stall, and William stepped over his mother's feet to take his place on her left. Going out [after the prayers], the boys chased after

their father, who dropped his surplice just outside the door, without looking round, into the hands of the pursuing butler, and again put his arms over the shoulders of his sons. (1948, p. 5)

Temple's biographer adds that the impression left on Temple's mind by these daily prayers never faded. Nor might it! Frederick Temple went on to become Archbishop of Canterbury (1897–1902), and in 1901 crowned Edward VII as the successor to Queen Victoria, with Frederick and William by his side as his attendants. (When William became Archbishop of Canterbury it was to be the only time a son would follow his father in that position.)[1]

Temple, then, was born in the heyday of Victorian England. Not only did his father become an archbishop but his mother was related to many members of the upper aristocracy; he grew up among the élite of a country whose empire was reaching the zenith of its power.

As a boy he received an education that instilled a strong intellectual self-confidence. He had learnt his Greek alphabet by the age of 10. As an 11- and 12-year-old he was already assessing the sermons he heard in church, and recording in his diary that most of them were 'excellent'. He was already offering advice to any who would hear it. In one boyish letter to his older brother, written when he had just heard that his older brother 'is learning to play', he wrote that Frederick will probably find that the organ will suit him best, and he must not mind if his fingers are a good deal stiffer than his younger brother's; the drudgery will soon be over but he should be careful not to let music interfere with his work. For the young William, his music master recommends that he should not start on the organ till he has learned to play quite perfectly on the piano all the scales: major, minor and chromatic. After this probably not very welcome advice, Temple then capped it all by signing himself 'Your loving brother, the musician of Fulham Palace (and Church music selector) William Temple'.

The teenage William went on to Rugby School, one of the most prestigious public schools of the time, and received a thorough academic education. He gained a grounding in the classics, philosophy, music and poetry. He was reading Kant and Mill by the age of 17. He imbibed the philosophical tradition of Thomas Arnold, who believed that the histories of Greece, Rome and Israel were three great steps forward on the path of the intellectual and moral development of humankind, and that modern Europe was the inheritor of all this: 'our life is in a manner a continuation of Greece, Rome and Israel', yet it 'exhibits a fuller development of the human race, a richer combination of the most remarkable elements'.[2] During the course of his life Temple would see the collapse of this self-confidently imperial view of history.

His study was encouraged and fired when he was at home. On one occasion he asked his father, 'Why do not philosophers rule the world? Would it not be a good thing if they did?' There was an impressively quick and emphatic answer from the elderly archbishop: 'They do rule it, silly, five hundred years after they are dead' (Iremonger, 1948, pp. 18–19). His schooling also included a not-very-distinguished record on the rugby field (though his bulk made him useful in a scrum), and walking trips to the Lake District. He was already developing a remarkable proficiency in the use of language in speaking and writing. When he left the school his headmaster wrote in his final report that he thought 'anything' was possible for Temple in the future.

In the event, he won an exhibition to Balliol College, Oxford, where he studied Greek and Latin literature and philosophy. He came under the influence of T. H. Green and his school. Green had been a philosophy tutor at the college in the 1870s, and had also been heavily involved in work for social reform in the poor districts of Oxford. He and those who followed him in the college believed that they were not training young men to be professional philosophers but to be public servants, in government, Church and law. The idealist philosophy they learnt, based ultimately on Hegel, saw human society within an historical context: the nation was caught up in a process of purposive growth, and the role of public servants was to work for the increasing realization of the perfect society that was slowly emerging. When Temple arrived at Balliol, the Scottish philosopher Edward Caird was head of the college and was continuing to teach this morally serious and empowering outlook. He called on the undergraduates to fulfil the duties 'of the station in which we stand', so that this present world may have 'its worth deepened . . . item by item, with all the elements that constitute it multiplied a hundred-fold in value, raised to a higher spiritual power'. Caird warned his listeners, though, that this ideal world would only be realized 'with persecutions'.[3] Temple was caught up in this challenging and progressive optimism and believed, like his peers, that he would have a significant role to play in the unfolding life of the nation.

He also developed a great love of literature. He embraced Keats, Shelley, Coleridge and Spenser. But he wrote that Milton's longer poems bored him stiff, and Shakespeare, while outstanding, had a 'pagan magnificence'.[4] With the George Eliot of *Romola* he found himself entirely out of sympathy. Robert Browning, on the other hand, he found to be a giant. Temple was drawn not only to Browning's style of writing but also to his underlying view of the world. In one of Temple's earliest published essays he described how he found Browning's writings fundamentally and thoroughly Christian: 'In both [Shakespeare and Browning] there is the joy of comedy, but in Browning only is there also the joy of work and worship.' 'To Browning', he also insists, 'the climax of history, the crown of philosophy, and the consummation of poetry is unquestionably the Incarnation' (Iremonger, 1948, p. 51). He confidently placed Browning with St John and Plato as being one of the three most formative influences upon his own thought (Temple, 1917a, p. vii).

He took a first-class degree and went on to become a lecturer in philosophy at Queen's College, Oxford, where he taught courses on Plato's philosophy (though there was more of Temple than Plato in his lectures). He harnessed his fluency with language in his teaching, and had the gift of being able to communicate what he had learned with a calm and infectious enthusiasm. He had also developed a great, though rather high-pitched, roistering laugh, one which seemed to shake the whole of his person and which endeared him to many, though it could infuriate others. And he developed his large waistline, having a lifelong passion for strawberry jam and strawberry ices. It was also his habit to finish the pudding while others moved on to the smoking of cigars. He later recounted how his white surplice, after being sent away to the cleaners, came back marked 'bell tent'!

Crossing class boundaries

William Temple was not just a bright young thing born of Rugby and Oxford, however: there was another side to him, a side exemplified in the fact that he came to be elected by the pioneering Workers' Educational Association (WEA) as its first president in

1908. This was the Temple who became aware of and angered by the conditions in which ordinary people were living at that time, and who become committed to working for a new and just social order. What brought about this growth, a growth from an upbringing at the heart of the English establishment to an adulthood committed to its reform?

First of all there was his innate openness as a human being. His manner was always relaxed, friendly and simple, wholly unpretentious, never 'rattled', never confrontational. He was, as Lancashire people would later say, utterly without 'side', and was able to give the whole of his attention to whoever he was speaking to. This was the foundation of all that followed.

Another stimulus to his social and intellectual development may have been his continual struggle with gout, a very painful recurrent illness that affected him in his feet and legs. The earliest attack occurred when he was just two years old, and he suffered intermittently from it until his death. As well as causing him pain, it would have made him sensitive to the struggles with disease faced by others and, especially, by the urban poor in an era before the founding of the National Health Service.

A further cause of growth was certainly the influence of Edward Caird. The distinguished Glaswegian philosopher had been sharply critical of the huge contrast between the living conditions of the Victorian suburbs and the slum tenements of that industrial city. When he came to Oxford he encouraged students to spend vacations at one of the Oxford houses in the East End of London. This Temple did, and he later recounted how, at his lodgings, 'there was a tin bed, rather rickety, and I lay on it with anxiety, for I always carried weight in every assembly. There was a tin wash-basin and a chair with three legs, upon which I read Bosanquet's *Logic*' (Iremonger, 1948, p. 43). It was all a bit of an adventure, of course, and it is doubtful whether the student houses did much for the people among whom they were placed. For Temple, though, it was a first step out of the confines of privilege and it led on to one of the most formative relationships of his life, the friendship with Albert Mansbridge, the founder of the WEA.

Temple was a young don at Queen's College when he met Mansbridge. He met him through his school and university friend R. H. Tawney, who persuaded Temple to attend the first national conference of the WEA in Oxford in 1905. The WEA was founded by the Co-operative Wholesale Society and the idea was that it would be very different from previous university-led initiatives (in which the workers had only to turn up at classes provided for them). This time the workers and university teachers would be equal partners in receiving and providing education. The initiative and planning would come from the workers' side, the academic learning and teaching from the university teachers. And it was all to be based on the recognition, according to Tawney, by

> the working-class movement that if it is to solve its own problems, mobilise its own forces, and create a social order more in conformity with its own ideals, it must attend to the education of its members with the same deliberation and per-sistence which it has brought to the improvement of their economic position. (Iremonger, 1948, p. 75)

Albert Mansbridge was an employee of the Co-op and it was through his vision, energy and perseverance that the WEA came into being and eventually succeeded. Through negotiation, persua-sion and inspiration he was able to get both the universities and the WEA to come together on a joint advisory committee to plan and supervise an educational programme for workers. His vision and his ability to reach across the bitter class divisions of Edwardian England was an inspiration to Temple. Temple later said, 'As a personal matter . . . he invented *me*' (Iremonger, 1948, p. 77).

Temple placed himself at the disposal of the WEA. He lectured around the country, speaking, for example, in Sheffield City Hall on 'the philosophic conception of liberty'. He took on committee work, being the co-secretary with Mansbridge of the tutorial classes committee. He wrote articles for the WEA in its journal *The Highway*. And, as mentioned, in 1908 he was elected its first presi-dent, an honour he regarded as the greatest in his life. Temple remained president until 1924.

All of this was important for Temple himself. Iremonger points out that, except for the butler at Fulham and Lambeth and his 'scouts' at Balliol and Queen's, he had hardly spoken to an adult 'handworker' till he joined the WEA. He had had no experience, for example, of the ordinary kind of home visiting undertaken by a parish priest. Nor had he yet lived in an industrial environment. Tawney describes the difference the WEA made to Temple:

The 'We and They' complex, which is so marked even among the most virtuous members of the privileged classes, might have clung to him as a habit, even though he knew it to be damnable in principle. It could not survive continuous co-operation with colleagues whose educational interests he shared, but whose experience of life was quite different from his own. (Iremonger, 1948, p. 88)

The contact with Mansbridge and the WEA was Temple's emancipation: it brought him into a wider, harsher but more vivid world where he discovered his own calling to the cause of social reform. It also formed the way he thought this reform should proceed: the experience of the WEA showed him that the majority did not want an overturning of the material and cultural riches previously enjoyed by the few, but the widening of their availability to all members of society. As far as education was concerned, for example, reform should involve extending to the majority the kind of education he had received at Oxford. In a presidential address to the WEA at their Oxford summer school in 1912 he touched on all of this:

For it is the WEA which has understood more definitely than any other body I am aware of, that what it finds of supreme value in the great centres of education [such as the ancient universities] is the spirit of the place rather than the instruction: and those of us who have received, or have been in a position to receive, the best that Oxford can give, and those of us who have had just a taste of her treasures in the [WEA] Summer School, will agree that Oxford does more for us than any lectures do. But while we say that, we need also to insist on a greater energy and efficiency, a greater and more living contact with the world of to-day in some, at least, of the centres of the old traditional type. (Iremonger, 1948, p. 83)

A call

William Temple's sense of his vocation developed in an emphatic way while he was an undergraduate at Balliol. He had always wanted to be ordained and to follow in the footsteps of his father, but during these years the sense of calling became more sharply focused and passionate. In a series of letters to close friends, reprinted in Iremonger's biography, Temple revealed the pattern of his thinking. The letters are full of the self-confidence already mentioned, but they do reveal some of the deepest concerns that would drive him forward. To his close friend John Stocks, in September 1901 or 1902, he confided that

> I mean that the Church – and consequently the nation – is in a very critical state: I mean that it is doing very nearly as much harm as good – and perhaps more. And this because of its narrow spirit . . . Our religion becomes more and more sensuous; preachers try to stir the emotions, not to direct the will. In short, anything more hostile to the New Testament than our modern English religion is hard to conceive. (Iremonger, 1948, p. 98)

Temple overstates the point but he goes on tellingly to describe the reasons for the harmful narrowness of his Church. The narrowness arose from an inability to adopt 'the spirit of criticism' within the Church. Temple meant by this a failure to rethink the Christian faith in the light of advances in scientific, philosophical and historical knowledge. *Essays and Reviews,* the controversial volume of essays of 1861, to which his father had contributed, had begun to apply critical ways of thinking to both the Bible and the creeds, but this needed to be continued in a more thoroughgoing way:

> Well, I believe that the only thing that can save us is a vigorous attack from within the Church on the existing conceptions of religion. While the Church is as it is, very few men of intellect *can* take orders: and until they do things cannot be much better. (Iremonger, 1948, p. 98)

Temple was trying to persuade John Stocks to be one of those who would offer themselves for ordination and take up the intellectual challenge. But in reality he was reflecting upon the reasons why he should enter the ordained ministry; he was also seeing that he was being called to commit himself to the intellectual reconstruction of the Christian faith.

But the malaise that Temple identified was not only intellectual, and so later in the same letter he wrote:

As a matter of practical politics – what is our so-called Christianity doing? Men are still encouraged to get drunk than otherwise; the poor are not housed, nor the naked clothed nor the hungry fed . . . the Church forgets that Christianity is not an attitude of mind, but a type of life: a man's spirit is known not by his opinion (creeds etc.) but by his actions and general conduct. (Iremonger, 1948, pp. 98–9)

Temple, then, was not just questioning the way the Christian faith was currently being understood and taught, but the whole way it was failing to respond to the social conditions of the time. Britain was the richest nation in the world, but a third of its population literally did not have enough to eat, had a life expectancy of a mere 30 years, and lived in slum conditions that led to 13,000 deaths a year from measles and over 7,000 deaths a year from diphtheria. Seebohm Rowntree's shocking and influential report on poverty in the city of York had been published only three years before, and Temple would have been aware of its findings. Temple's letters show that he believed the Church should have been confronting such social injustice. In a letter to another friend in May 1901 he put this view in an historical context:

The Church has been roused – by Wesley and others – to a new spiritual devotion: and to a new sense of beauty as an expression of this devotion by Newman: so we have got the devotion and its formal expression: the most important part remains – namely to put that behind all actions whatever, and identify religion with life. (Iremonger, 1948, p. 100)

Temple was thinking of the epistle of James and applying its argument (that faith without good works was dead) to his own day. In another letter to John Stocks in October 1902 he wrote that 'we have to teach S. James' doctrine' and that anyone who is not interested in '"good works" is in effect anti-Christ'. After this startling statement he went on to show the kind of view of Christ that he believed was now needed to underpin everything else:

The Christ men believe in and worship is to a great extent a myth and an idol – very different from Him who lived and died 'to bear witness to the truth', and Whose Spirit lived and

spoke in Socrates and Buddha and Mahomet [*sic*] as it did
also in Hosea and Luther and Browning. Men do not realize
that Christ requires a good life and not church-going, and
knowledge of God more than communicating . . . (Iremonger,
1948, pp. 102–3)

And so it was not only the current theology and practice of the
Church of England that Temple was questioning, but also the traditional understanding of Christ found in most churches. He was
wanting to abandon the idea that Christ can be found only in
institutional Christianity, and was advocating an inclusivist understanding of Christ's presence in the world: the Lord does not
belong only within narrow ecclesiastical circles, but to all humanity,
and poor as well as rich. At the end of one letter, summing it all up,
he wrote that

I know I am right in this, though I may exaggerate the evil: I
don't think so however – and if I lived 700 years before Christ
I should call it the word of the Lord. I don't know whether
Amos actually saw things – probably not: but his vision is
mine – 'I saw the Lord standing above the altar' (His own altar
it was) 'and He said unto me, SMITE!' (Iremonger, 1948,
p. 100)

These youthful letters do not represent Temple's mature understanding of the Christian faith: he would become more orthodox in
his view of Christ as he got older. But they do reveal underlying
passions that would remain with him throughout his adult life: the
conviction of the need for a restatement of the Christian faith that
was intellectually credible; an anger and protest at the harsh social
conditions of the time; the commitment to reforming the Church
so that it practised what it preached; and the belief in a Christ who
was not confined by human divisions but was the Lord of all and
present with all. And these letters reveal how he felt the underlying
call, to him as to others, was the call to prophecy, to be like Amos or
Hosea: to be a herald and instrument of a new world, by graphically
setting before Church and nation the judging ideal of God's
kingdom, so that they would move towards it.

Such passionate concerns and the sense of divine call that arose
out of them explain the boundless yet focused energy of Temple's

subsequent career: they show why he developed his extended interest in theological restatement through an engagement with the philosophy of the day; they explain his long-standing commitment to social and educational reform, as strong at the end of his life as at the beginning; they explain his involvement with church reform, a cause that might otherwise seem at odds with his other interests; and they account for his commitment to ecumenical bridge-building, an aspect of his work that became increasingly important. These early letters, when read in the light of his subsequent career, reveal the inner vision that drove him forward: they show that he was a man with a calling, a calling given to him while he was an undergraduate.

But the question that we must pose within the context of his life, and within the analysis in the coming pages, is whether he actually became a prophet? Did he come to graphically set God's reign before nation as well as Church, so that they moved towards it, or did other pressures divert him from a true realization of his vocation? He undoubtedly became a significant leader of the Church and a voice heard by the nation, but did he finally rise to the challenge of being a prophetic herald and instrument of God's judgement and salvation?

Trauma

Temple's first attempt to respond to this call created the first major upset of his life. The catalyst was his own less than orthodox early understanding of the Christian faith. When he took up the philosophy lectureship at Queen's College he spent some months on a sabbatical study leave in Germany. He wrote the following letter from Jena in 1905:

> I do honestly wish, though of course I don't do it, to 'confess Jesus Christ as Lord', and I believe that I am capable of, and definitely experience, what is called 'communion' with Him. I am inclined, I think honestly, to assent to the Virgin Birth, though I am pretty clear that it ought not to be in the creed, because it fastens attention on the wrong point. But it is hard to be really honest! (Iremonger, 1948, p. 106)

This was an unusual and uncomfortable state in which Temple found himself. As one of life's great enthusiasts he was used to being very positive about the things that interested him. But here, he was caught by a cleft stick of convictions: on the one side his philosophical beliefs suggested that the virgin birth and bodily resurrection of Christ should not be regarded as foundational to the Christian faith, and on the other side his long-standing vocation called him to a kind of ministry which required his assent to such doctrines. He was used to being emphatic about his beliefs, but now he did not know what to think. He took time to decide what to do, talking with friends and consulting with colleagues. But by January 1906 he reached the point where he thought he could proceed to ordination, and he wrote to the Bishop of Oxford, Francis Paget, asking to be sponsored. He included some statements of what he believed but, dangerously, wrote, 'I am very conscious that my opinions are still subject to considerable change. In the statements I sent I stated definitely conclusions to which I am led by very slight preponderance of argument in some cases' (Iremonger, 1948, p. 109).

He was not prepared for Paget's response of 3 February 1906. The Bishop, a High Churchman who was not normally unsympathetic with attempts to marry Christian doctrine with modern ways of thinking, quoted this statement back to Temple and put a road block in his path:

> Weighing these words I have to say, with all respect, and with sorrow, and anxiety lest I may be judging amiss, that I could not take the responsibility of ordaining to the Ministry of the Church of England, and sending forth as a teacher in its Name, one who, in regard to those two main points of history which I believe to be essential to, inextricable from our Creed, stands on such uncertain, precarious, unsteady ground. (Iremonger, 1948, p. 109)

It must have taken some courage on Paget's part to say this to a son of an Archbishop of Canterbury who, in so many other ways, was brilliantly qualified for ordination. But say it he did and, perhaps for the first time in his life, Temple found that things were not going the way he expected. He wrote to his friend John Stocks that it was 'a most tremendous disappointment I confess'. The same letter also shows Temple writing, 'there are nasty elements in my disappointment – including the annoyance of a frustrated ambition to hear my sermons praised! . . . But I had hoped to do useful work as a parson, and thought my gifts (!) peculiarly suited to that kind of work' (Iremonger, 1948, p. 112). He resigned himself to reforming the Church 'from the outside' as an Oxford philosopher. The letter shows that Temple was already beginning to grow in self-awareness.

During the following summer his criticisms of the Church remained undimmed:

> More and more I come to regard 'Churchiness' as a survival of the useless: it was necessary once; without the Dogmatism and ecclesiasticism of the early mediaeval church the whole of Christianity would have gone into smoke. But the walls built to protect now only confine and cramp, and should be pulled down. (Iremonger, 1948, p. 114)

Temple added, ruefully, that 'it is better not to try a movement [of reform] outside the Church, but inside it. [But] If the Church turns one out one must go on outside.'

He had to wait. In the meantime he continued with his lecturing and with his work for the WEA. He also had short stays at the Bermondsey Medical Mission in the docklands area of London, assisting Dr Stansfeld with his medical and missionary work. And he became involved with the Student Christian Movement in 1907, attending their summer conferences. At one gathering, attended by 800 students from a wide range of churches, he heard Henry Scott Holland address the conference. He wrote that 'the thing that really lives with me is Scott Holland's extraordinary oration on the power of Christ to regenerate society here or anywhere else.' It seems that Scott Holland, who combined an inspiring radical political commitment with an orthodox Christian faith, had an important formative influence on Temple at this time. Iremonger suggests that Holland guided him to the conviction that 'the Catholic Faith does not consist of a number of separate articles or formulae, but is a coherent whole. It is one structure.' So, Holland's argument ran, if there were aspects of the faith that you knew by experience to be true, the 'intervening' ones could be accepted, even taken for granted, just because they belong to the integrity of the whole (see Iremonger, 1948, pp. 125–6). Iremonger suggests that between 1906 and 1908 Temple's own Christian thinking moved in this direction, away from the philosopher's analytic approach to the theologian's integrative approach, accepting and then seeking to interpret the faith as a whole.

By the middle of 1908 he was again ready to approach a bishop. This time he wrote to Randall Davidson, the then Archbishop of Canterbury, who had the right to occasionally ordain academics outside the diocesan structures. Temple went to see him and, afterwards, described Davidson as being 'the essence of kindness and sanity – without a glimmer of inspiration'. But Davidson decided that Temple should be ordained and undertook to square the circle with Paget. There followed an unfailingly polite and painstaking correspondence between the two, during which Temple had to make another visit to Davidson.[5] Paget at first refused to give his blessing to the proposal. Davidson wrote again and this time informed Paget that he would ordain Temple. Rank, it seems, was being pulled. But Paget did, at this point, give his unqualified blessing to the proposal.

Temple could at last sit the exams for ordination, and he was made a deacon by Davidson in Canterbury Cathedral in December 1908, and a priest during the same month in 1909. It was the end of the beginning for this rising star.

In his deacon's year he prepared and delivered a set of addresses to the Student Christian Movement in London. They were published in a volume aptly named (for him) *The Faith and Modern Thought*. In those lectures he spoke about the grounds for believing in God, the place of revelation in the believer's life, and the historic basis for Christianity. At the point in the argument where he described the place of Christ in God's purposes a question naturally arises for us: what about his views on the virgin birth and the bodily resurrection of Christ? These were the credal beliefs that had caused him some soul searching and grief in 1905 and 1906: how did he handle them now?

The virgin birth was not mentioned: it would not be until he was a parish priest in London, in 1915 or 1916, that he would come to certain belief in that, during a symphony concert at the Queen's Hall! But in the lectures the resurrection was given some prominence:

If we are to be on sure ground in taking [Christ] as the revelation of the Divine, it is necessary that the Divine Power should be seen clearly co-operating with Him, carrying Him through

His ultimate self-surrender, and bringing Him out victorious. We need the Resurrection. (Temple, 1910, pp. 76–7)

The resurrection, therefore, was now central to Temple's thinking. But what of the bodily resurrection of Jesus? At this point his thinking was not quite so emphatic. Assuming a Platonic distinction between body and spirit, Temple wrote that after the resurrection:

what matters is that the Lord was alive. As far as I can see it does not matter very much what became of His Body. I do not doubt that His Body was in some way risen and glorified; but if anybody finds this incredible, that need not prevent him from believing in the reality of the Lord's Resurrection. That the Lord was alive seems to me certain. (Temple, 1910, pp. 79–80)

Paget would probably have found this position still too uncertain, precarious and unsteady. Temple had moved, but not all the way. The Church, though, in the person of Archbishop Davidson, had also moved, towards Temple, and the result had been his ordination. Temple was still only teaching what he himself could believe with honesty and integrity, but for the Church it was now enough.

The trauma of being turned down by Paget, then, resulted in Temple's inner growth in a number of ways. It gave him a rare experience of failure. It led him to further reflection on the Christian faith and a more integrated understanding of its nature. It led, also, to a growth in self-awareness. It must have also increased his understanding and sympathy with others who also experienced failure (as a diocesan bishop he would later be very lenient with wayward clergy). But it did not result in him abandoning his passionate concern for restating the Christian faith in intellectually persuasive terms for the time. *The Faith and Modern Thought* shows that this ambition was still very much alive and, as we shall see, it would provide the motivating force behind his influential teaching ministry.

CHAPTER 2

Search for a Role

Distracted headmastering

The years at Oxford created an inner conflict within Temple. On the one hand his church establishment upbringing, schooling and university education created one set of expectations among those around him, and within his own thinking. His moving from undergraduate life at Balliol to the lectureship at Queen's College conformed very well to such expectations. His intellectual interests in philosophy, literature and music were of a piece with them, as was his ordination as a deacon and priest within the Church of England. The expected course for such a talented and promising young man, following the revered example of his father, would have been to become a headmaster of one of the prestigious public schools of the time, and then perhaps a bishop or other senior cleric within the established Church.

But Temple had discovered different ambitions within himself. He had become very critical of his Church, accusing it of hypocrisy and regarding it as doing more harm than good within the nation. He had become offended and angered by the conditions in which ordinary people were living at that time, and he wanted to do something about them. And he had become critical of the way the Christian faith was being understood and taught: an intellectually rigorous reconstruction of belief was needed. Then, as we saw, Temple also came into contact with the Workers' Educational Association: this not only gave him contact with independently minded working people but also showed him that his presence and contribution within that movement was wanted and valued. The possibility of a prophetic ministry had opened up to him, one that would sometimes bring him into conflict with the church establishment, and he felt deeply drawn towards it.

The reality of the conflict between these two 'futures' was seen in the trauma of his being refused ordination by Paget. His upbringing and desire to follow his father had made him offer himself for ordination. But his radical ambitions had made him rethink the Christian faith in an honest and rigorous way, and this had led him to state his beliefs in a way which Paget found too uncertain. When Paget refused to sponsor Temple we saw how deeply disappointed he was. Other young men might have reacted differently, seeing such a refusal as a release and an opportunity to follow other ambitions. Temple did not find it resolved anything: the conflict was within his own being.

Now, at the point in his life where he *had* been ordained and must decide which way to go, the conflict reappeared. He learnt that the governors of Repton School, a well-known public school near Burton-on-Trent, were to elect a new headmaster and that some governors thought that he should stand. Here was an opportunity to follow in his father's footsteps, not to Rugby School but to one very similar. His first response was to visit the school and weigh it all up. But, just before the election, he wrote to the outgoing head that he believed he should stay where he was in Oxford: 'I am sure I am meant to go on for a time as at present . . . I must ask you not to bring my name before the Governors to-morrow.'[6] His friends were also advising him not to go to Repton but, if he was to move, to go to a parish in the East End of London.

On his way to Australia, where he was to lecture to a number of Student Christian Unions, he heard that he had nevertheless been elected! He was now in a quandary. Those closest to him had advised him to stay where he was. His ambitions lay in a direction very different from running public schools. But the 'establishment path' was opening up to him and he felt its pull. He was given a deadline by which to reply. Twenty years later, speaking at a mission to Oxford University, he described how he came to the decision:

. . . having weighed up the question as carefully as I could – and we must always do that – and having come to no conclusion at all, I began at eight o'clock in the evening to say my prayers, and for three hours, without a pause, I tried to concentrate all my desires on knowing clearly what was God's Will for me. I do not know how those three hours went; they did not seem very long; but when eleven o'clock struck I knew perfectly well what I had got to do, and that was to accept; and I have never had a shadow of doubt since that it was right. (Iremonger, 1948, pp. 134–5)

The impressive seriousness with which Temple came to this decision suggests that it was right. However, the time at Repton was not a success. Even during the month when Temple took up the post he was writing to his brother that he doubted whether headmastering was really his line (Iremonger, 1948, p. 128). When he wrote to a friend explaining why he had accepted the post he did not say that the main reason was the running of a school or the desire to teach boys but, rather, the opportunity for furthering his views and hopes for English education through the Headmasters' Conference (Iremonger, 1948, p. 134). Such an ambition would take him out of the school rather than into it. And then, once he had arrived, everyone was expecting great changes in the running of the place. To the previous head he had written that the Public Schools 'seemed to me to reproduce our class-divisions in accentuated form, and that I should hope, after learning the ropes, to find ways of moving towards a system which would tend to diminish them' (Iremonger, 1948, p. 147). The teachers came to expect a minor revolution, but nothing seemed to happen once he had arrived at the school. Sunday afternoon piano recitals were introduced, new hymns were sung at the chapel services, and an attempt was made to introduce a house-tutor system, but the teachers opposed that idea and it was dropped. As term followed term it became apparent there was to be no revolution after all. (He later explained that he had learnt that institutions should be run on their own lines or else be scrapped – they could not be turned in new directions and run with the same power as before. See Iremonger, 1948, p. 148.) As time went on, Temple seemed to be away from the school more and more with speaking and preaching engagements elsewhere (and writing essays for the volume *Foundations,* on which more below). Finally, by the time he left the school it was clear that the place had not been prospering under his headship. There was 'a fearful crop of failures' among the students, and Temple admitted that while he may have been good for the more mature boys he was 'not good with the general ruck' (Iremonger, 1948, p. 128). After just two years and three months in the job the Archbishop of Canterbury, Davidson, asked him to be Rector of St Margaret's, Westminster, with an attached canonry at Westminster Abbey. Temple had little hesitation in accepting the post, though when it was discovered that a canon was required to have been a priest for at least six years, he had to withdraw. He returned to Repton, but only for another year and a half .

In the light of all of this we could ask why God had led Temple to Repton. One answer may be that Temple was purposely led into a cul-de-sac. The example of his father had been a powerful influence and had resulted in William going to the same institutions as his father, in particular Rugby and Balliol. It had also made headmastership seem the right kind of thing for him to do, for his father had been a distinguished headmaster of Rugby. William may have needed to discover that following the footsteps of his father was not the way forward for his career, and that he needed to discover his own path. The undistinguished time at Repton would have shown him the need to be his own person.[7]

A roving rector

What, though, was the right way forward? In a letter to the staff at Repton Temple described his reasons for leaving the school and taking up an appointment as Rector of St James' Church, Piccadilly, in London. The letter, inauspiciously, does not suggest that the reason for moving was the call to parish ministry but something else entirely:

> The reason that has chiefly weighed with me is this: during the last year I have been drawn more and more into the current of general Church politics and have felt wholly unable to resist; I have been made a member of three new Committees whose work is of central and urgent importance. But my work here has prevented my doing for those Committees the work which was really called for, while the interest of the problems with which they are concerned has drawn my attention some-what seriously away from school and its needs. I trust that the school has not yet suffered from this, but it would suffer

before long. I have therefore felt bound to accept the offer of a position where I can respond to the claims made upon me without feeling that my primary duty is being neglected. Of the feelings to which this decision gives rise in myself I will not now attempt to speak. (Iremonger, 1948, p. 151)

To accept a parish incumbency because it will provide a base from which to work outside the parish does not suggest Temple had found the role he was searching for. He was clearly more interested in national church affairs than in any more locally based kind of ministry, and this indicates that he would not be at St James' for very long.

Nor was he. Just over three years later he was moving to another post. And while he was at St James' he did not enter into parish ministry with any great enthusiasm. With the exception of his preaching he 'was not the stuff of which parish priests are made' (Iremonger, 1948, p. 168). He was not good at small talk with strangers, he had little experience of the mundane difficulties and worries of ordinary people, and he did not enjoy house-to-house visiting around the parish. In this respect St James' did not prove too demanding as there were relatively few homes in a mainly commercial area of London; added to this he had two curates and a parish worker who could carry out the routine work of the parish. It was clear that being a parish priest was not his vocation and, because Britain was now at war with Germany, his kind of reasoned presentation of the Christian faith from the pulpit was not likely to make the impact it otherwise would. Temple's search for a role had to continue.

His gout recurred at this time, as well. In a letter to a friend he described how his doctor was encouraging him to lose weight and to hold his body

in the right position. I believe in him because, after looking at me for a moment, he said 'Of course every time you take a lot of exercise, you are making your stoutness worse' – which is quite true. My fattening periods have always been those when I took most exercise. (Iremonger, 1948, p. 170)

But he remained 'stout' for the rest of his life, and his gout remained a recurrent companion to the end.

Nevertheless, unsatisfactory as they were, the years at St James' were also very creative and formed the foundation of much that followed. Living at the heart of the capital and near the centre of national life Temple could not avoid contact with some of the most stark and disturbing issues of the time. He could not avoid, for example, speaking on the morality of the First World War and the role of the churches within the nation. He was not a pacifist: he believed that Britain had a duty to be involved in the war in Europe. But nor would he, unlike most of the clergy at the beginning of the war, act as a recruiting sergeant for the armed forces. Unlike his diocesan bishop in London, Winnington-Ingram, he did not preach 'war sermons' designed to generate a kind of jingoistic patriotism that would make young men join up.

As the war progressed and the horror and waste at the front became widely known, many people began to question how the God who allowed this to take place could also be a God of love. Temple described this in a 1916 sermon at St James':

the blow fell, and many were much shaken in their belief in any God of love; and those who had never held any such belief asked how, in face of the events of these days, we could without hypocrisy maintain such a belief.

There were two typical responses. One, typical of many preachers, was to simplistically equate the coming of the war with the judgement of God: the suffering and carnage was specially sent by God as punishment for the wrongdoings of Europe. The other was to abandon belief in God altogether. Temple did neither. In a sermon at St James' he showed how it was possible to hold together the belief that the war was caused by human actions rather than by God's intervention, with the view that there was nevertheless an element of divine punishment in what was happening. From the pulpit at St James' he spoke of how he had heard people 'during this war speak about it as if God had deliberately caused the war in order to punish mankind for certain sins'. He reported that they usually named drunkenness or impurity or Sabbath-breaking as the sins in question. He continued:

I venture to say that is sheer superstition. We can trace the actual causes of the war, and we know quite well that its

causes were in human wills, and we are not at liberty to say
that God intervened in the history of the world to inflict
anguish and pain by means of the war as punishment for
certain sins that have no relation to it. How could the war
grow out of drunkenness? All the way through this Gospel of
St John we are taught that a judgement of God is not a deliberate act of His intervening in the world to make guilty people
suffer, but an automatic product of His Presence and Revelation.

So the war was not a deliberate judgement of God upon the world.
Nevertheless, it was a judgement upon the sin of nations in an
indirect way:

> The sin which led immediately to the outbreak of war we may
> believe to be mainly in one nation, but the root is to be found
> among all peoples, and not only among those who are
> fighting, but neutral peoples just as much. The punishment
> for that sin comes through the moral order which God has set
> up in the world, an order which reacts upon those who break
> it. So that if a man persists in doing what is contrary to the will
> of God, in doing evil which he has himself recognized as such,
> the consequences of his sin will at last overtake him. God has
> no pleasure in the infliction of that penalty, the penalty is
> rather a warning against indulging in the evil course at all. The
> pleasure of God is in men's salvation; men's salvation is His
> purpose. (Iremonger, 1948, pp. 174–5)

And so through all the shattering carnage and seeming hopeless-
ness it might still be possible to believe in a loving creator who has
given to the world a moral order, an order intended to lead to the
salvation of all people. Human nature, in this order, has the
freedom to accept or reject this moral order; and the First World
War, for Temple, was a consequence of a massive rejection of that
order. But the possibility of conforming to the moral order and
finding a wonderful salvation was still open. In these few words,
Temple was able to outline the kind of realistic yet inspiring Christian ethical viewpoint that would become the secret of his moral
leadership in the country in the inter-war years.

Temple described the war years as 'harder days than we had

known' and he spoke of needing 'the strong authority of the Judge of men . . . the Christ of the New Testament, the Christ whom we had forgotten, the Christ who rules whether we would have it or not' (Iremonger, 1948, p. 175). And for him the place where he found this Christ was, above all, the fourth Gospel. Beginning with the congregation at St James', and continuing with ordinands at Manchester, York and Canterbury, and with other gatherings of clergy and laity, he began to speak about and reflect on this Gospel, meditating on its obscurities and finally publishing his *Readings in St John's Gospel* in 1939 and 1940. The earliest form of his readings comes from the years at St James'.

He also edited a Church of England weekly newspaper, *The Challenge*, from July 1915 to the autumn of 1918. This was a paper dedicated to expressing 'the challenge offered by the cross of Christ to worldliness and indifference'. It claimed to be independent of all party matters in Church and state, though others would describe it as having a liberal tone in its theology, in its general outlook and in its desire to see church reform bringing in a greater role for the laity in church affairs. Temple would write leaders while sitting in the board meetings of the paper, or in railway station waiting rooms, or in the early hours after addressing meetings around the country. The paper advocated the right to conscientious objection. When considering the question of whether such objection to joining the armed forces was legitimate, he wrote that 'The individual must, of course, follow his own conscience, which means simply his deliberate judgement with regard to the right course for him to follow.' And when there is conflict with the will of the state 'what is to happen? First and foremost, there should be on each side absolute respect for the other. We must recognise the fallibility of the human conscience not only in the other man, but also in ourselves.'[8] And so he became critical of many tribunals that adopted a contemptuous approach to those objecting to conscription.

The Challenge idealistically advocated total prohibition of alcohol for the duration of the war, but it also called for a living wage for every worker, for educational reform so that every child in the country would benefit, and for church reform. One member of the board described the paper as a somewhat amateurish affair, with none of its managing group knowing anything about the technique of journalism. But they 'plunged' along, and Temple's editorship gave the paper a direction and a theological weight.

He was also heavily involved with the National Mission of 1916, an unsuccessful campaign of meetings and church services to attract the general population back to church, as well as the WEA, YMCA, British Association (as chairman of the education section), and much else. The roving and breathless character of his life at this time (and more or less of the rest of his life) is seen in a letter to his brother:

> here are my activities of the last fortnight. Oct. 8, Two sermons here. 9, Speech at Tottenham. 10, To Southwell. 11, To Nottingham: Sermon and Speech. 12, To Manchester: two sermons. 13, Three sermons in Manchester. Back to London. 14, Demonstration in Hyde Park. 15, Two sermons here. 16, Variety of Committees. 17, Three Committees. 18, To Ludlow: two sermons. 19, To Bridgnorth: two addresses – then to Hereford, and three addresses there. 20, To London: visited Nana for tea. 21, Quiet Day for teachers: 3 sermons. 22, Sermon here in morning: at Christ's Hospital (Horsham) in evening. 23, Two committees . . . So life is rather a strain! (Iremonger, 1948, pp. 190–1)

These years also saw the death of his mother, who had kept home for him in Oxford, Repton and in London. She died, at the age of 69, early in the morning on Good Friday in 1915. Temple was due to lead the Three Hours Service that day and was determined that his parishioners should be allowed to keep the day without being distracted by what had just happened. So the news was kept within the house and, despite having just lost his closest companion, he led the service as planned. He later described himself as 'numbed' by the blow. His biographer describes the year that followed as the loneliest in his life.

During the following year, however, he was able to get to know Frances Anson, who worked at *The Challenge* offices. Temple's biographer says very little about his close personal relationships. We can only conjecture about this side of his life, and when Iremonger reaches the point in the story where Temple and Frances Anson become engaged he seems more interested in the connections between her family and his family than in the actual courtship of the couple. All we are told is that Temple wrote to Mrs Anson asking for permission to marry her daughter, and that they were engaged in May 1916. But Temple's own words to his brother after the engagement hint at rather more:

> I thought I should be excited, and of course I was before the final interview; but from that moment there has been simply a sense of floating on a quite calm sea of contentment and happiness – with the water deliciously warm so that one need never get out. (Iremonger, 1948, p. 199)

On the night before the marriage Temple, famously, sat late into the night finishing his book *Mens Creatrix*. He and Frances were married on 24 June 1916 in St James', with an address from the Archbishop of Canterbury, Davidson. On the honeymoon Temple read aloud his favourite Browning poems to his new wife, but he also suffered a bad attack of hay fever (the cottage where they were staying was opposite a hayfield in full flower). The holiday also included a visit to Repton School, where Temple preached, and to Alington School, where he also preached.

Many of the events of these years suggest that the presence and example of his father (who had died when he was an undergraduate in 1902) were never far away, but what happened next in his career suggests that his own radical ambitions were able to reassert themselves.

Mixing philosophy with theology

The finishing of *Mens Creatrix* is a reminder of another of Temple's deeply held ambitions, of restating the Christian faith in an intellectually credible way. Did he begin to fulfil this ambition during this fourth decade of his life? There were two places where he certainly made an attempt to do so, the first being his contribution to the volume of essays written by a group of Oxford scholars and published in 1912 as *Foundations,* and the second being this book of 1917.

The 1912 volume was subtitled 'A Statement of Christian Belief in Terms of Modern Thought'. It was written as a response to modern gains in scientific knowledge, such as the acceptance of the theory of evolution and the rise of the critical study of ancient documents. It was the third volume from Oxford-based scholars that attempted to do this: the first had been *Essays and Reviews* in 1861 and the second *Lux Mundi* in 1889. The writers, who included B. H. Streeter and Walter Moberly, set themselves the task of re-examining and, if need be, restating the foundations of their belief 'in the light of the knowledge and thought of the day'. Temple wrote a long essay on the divinity of Christ and a shorter one on the Church.[9]

It was all wittily summed up by Ronald Knox, a conservative theologian who was about to become a Roman Catholic, as 'How much will Jones swallow?' In other words, Christian belief was restated so as not to go beyond what Jones, 'a modern cultivated man', may find acceptable. The problem, for Knox, was that the 'modern cultivated man' was increasingly not finding any religious belief acceptable, so such an approach was bound to leave increasingly little on the table. Temple wrote a long and illuminating letter back to Knox (reprinted in Iremonger, 1948). The nub of what he wrote was this: 'I am not a spiritual doctor trying to see how much Jones can swallow and keep down: I am more respectable than that; *I am Jones himself asking what there is to eat*' (p. 162). In other words, Temple was making no apology for identifying himself with the modern mind in all its questionings. Knox, like many others who were more obviously orthodox (whether Catholic or Evangelical), as Adrian Hastings points out, had emphatically rejected the package of modern culture.[10] Temple and his fellow essayists were committed to trying to marry that modern culture with the Christian faith.

His contributions to *Foundations*, though, were surprisingly orthodox. Whereas Streeter, for example, went some way to embracing Albert Schweitzer's questioning of the bodily resurrection of Christ, Temple in his essay did not question the doctrine of the incarnation. For him, Christ was God, and this was not so much a question as an answer to many questions: 'The wise question is not "Is Christ Divine?" but, "What is God like?" And the answer to that is "Christ"' (Temple, 1912c, p. 259). Temple's contribution was more significant in the route he used to get to this point, a route through philosophy. What is the relation, he asked, of Christ to the Father? 'It is clear that no final answer can be given until philosophy has provided us with a final account of Personality, both Human and Divine' (Temple, 1912c, p. 248). His essay, though, did not go very far in exploring what this philosophical account might be. Such an account would occur in his first major book.

Mens Creatrix was this book, a philosophical study of 'creative mind'. It is a heady brew of philosophy, theology, poetry and political thought. It had been planned in 1908 when he had been lecturing in philosophy at Queen's College, and had been written in odd moments at Oxford, Repton and in London. More than half of it, he admitted, was dictated in spare half-hours at St James'. Temple modestly described its 370 pages as 'a stimulus, if it may be so, to some real philosopher to do more adequately what I am only able to sketch out'. Nevertheless, the book is a serious contribution to philosophical enquiry. It tries, ambitiously, to show how the kinds of questions raised by philosophy, especially the philosophies of knowledge, art and ethics, can be answered by religion, which is described as the culmination of science, art and morality, and in particular by the incarnation of Christ. In the prologue he described the book in the following colourful way:

> We shall watch the Creative Mind of Man as it builds its Palace of Knowledge, its Palace of Art, its Palace of Civilisation, its Palace of Spiritual Life. And we shall find that each edifice is incomplete in a manner that threatens its security. Then we shall see that the Creative Mind of God, in whose image Man was made, has offered the Revelation of Itself to be the foundation of all that the Human Mind can wish to build. Here is the security we seek; here, and nowhere else. 'Other foundation can no man lay than that which is laid, which is Jesus Christ.' (Temple, 1917a, p. 4)

Temple was quite clear, however, that reasoned argument alone would not prove the case he was trying to make: 'Yet even at the last the security is of Faith and not of Knowledge; it is not won by intellectual grasp but by personal loyalty; and its test is not in logic only, but in life' (Temple, 1917a, p. 4). The living of the Christian way, in other words, was the only sure route to knowing the truth of Christianity.

The argument of *Mens Creatrix* was based on the idealist philosophy Temple had learnt at Oxford, from Edward Caird and, through him, T. H. Green. It sought to show how the natural sciences, art (including drama and poetry) and morality, were activities that could be seen as exhibiting different facets of Mind, an all-encompassing reality that showed there was an underlying unity behind these different activities. For Temple, the reality of Mind had evolved through an organic and unfolding process of evolution and, within that, human history. The earliest and most primitive forms of life were not sentient, they were not thinking beings. Only towards the end of the evolutionary process, when humanity came into being, did Mind emerge. It was responsible for the achievements of human culture, not least the cultures of Greece, Rome and Palestine (as Thomas Arnold had argued). Temple believed that Mind was the goal towards which evolution had been moving: it was also the thing which had been drawing evolution to this goal. The full disclosure of Mind would therefore provide the key to reality, though philosophy itself was unable to find this disclosure.

At this point in the argument Temple had prepared the ground for his presentation of Christ as the incarnation of Mind:

> The whole process of that revelation which has been going on through nature, through history and through prophets, comes to complete fulfilment in the Incarnation . . . Only in the life of Christ is this manifestation given. What we see in Him is what we should see in the history of the universe if we could apprehend that history in its completeness. (Temple, 1917a, pp. 317–18)

And for Temple, the fourth Gospel came closest to expressing this mystery when it declared that 'The Word was made flesh and we beheld His glory.'

Mens Creatrix has been criticized for a number of reasons. The philosopher Dorothy Emmet commented that in spite of its clarity of style and exposition it

> is a curiously disjointed book. It bears the marks of having been dictated in odd half-hours . . . It passes quickly from one large topic to another: from idealist logic to discussions of art, tragedy, ethics, international and social politics, and Christian theology, without the ground gained at each stage being established sufficiently firmly to bear much searching criticism.' (Iremonger, 1948, p. 523)

Even more seriously, the discussion of evil, which occupies the longest chapter in the book, is not as convincing as it needed to be.

The existence of evil in the world was obviously a problem for Temple's argument. How could the evolution of the world be the purposeful unfolding of Mind when there was clearly so much that was so terribly wrong, not least the carnage taking place on the fields of Flanders when the book was published. Temple recognized the problem of evil and grappled deeply with it. But his solution could not finally answer the problem. He argued that the existence of evil served a greater purpose: with human suffering, for example, there was often a positive good that could come out of it:

> Pain, coupled with fortitude in its endurance, especially when this is inspired by love, and meeting the full sympathy which at first lightens it and at last destroys it by removal of its grounds, is sometimes the condition of what is best in human life. (Temple, 1917a, p. 278)

He admitted that this could not be seen with all cases of human suffering in the world. J. W. Rogerson, in a sympathetic discussion of Temple's philosophical thought, asks what of the suffering of the concentration camps, a suffering arising out of an evil that was so appalling it could never be justified by any future outcome? Temple could only write that:

> All we can claim is that we have found a principle on which, where we can trace its operation, suffering becomes a necessary element in the full goodness of the world; that in some cases this principle can actually be traced; that in others its action must be assumed if we are to maintain the rationality of the world. (Temple, 1917a, p. 281)

Rogerson says, though, that he could never

> have encouraged the inmates of Auschwitz or Buchenwald with the thought that *their* suffering was a necessary part of purposeful reality and that good was bound to come from it – indeed, that the world would ultimately be a poorer place without the opportunities which concentration camps provided for overcoming evil with good.

He, and many others, in the face of evil, prefer *not* to maintain the rationality of the world.[11] The world cannot be as unified and purposeful as *Mens Creatrix* argued. Indeed Temple himself, as we shall see later, came finally to acknowledge the irrationality of the world.

Mens Creatrix, then, did not achieve the arranged marriage of philosophy with theology which Temple had sought. As he had suspected (when writing the preface) he had not, after all, been able to rise to the challenge of presenting an adequate philosophical theology. Consequently his role in the service of Christ, it seems, was not to be primarily as an academic philosopher. Nevertheless, he would return to the writing of philosophical theology on two more occasions in his life, and each time more successfully than the last. All was not lost, by any means.

Campaigning for change

Temple was well aware that the National Mission of 1916 had largely failed in its objectives of reconverting the nation, and the reasons were not difficult to see: the war had shown the Church of England to be largely out of touch with the lives of the ordinary working people whose sons were now dying for their country in the trenches. If the gospel was to be heard, the body proclaiming it would need to be reformed and many ancient abuses removed. There were remarkable anomalies in the way the Church was run: a priest in one parish of 850 people received an income of over £6,000 a year, while in a neighbouring parish another priest who ministered to 19,000 people received £400 a year, and other clergy received much less. A campaign was needed to free the Church from its identification with the anachronistic establishment of the past.

The 'Life and Liberty' movement arose out of the recognition that if the Church was to be reformed it needed self-government. Up to this point in the Church of England there had been no General Synod or Church Assembly, no parochial church councils or electoral rolls, let alone deanery or diocesan synods. All changes in ecclesiastical law and practice had had to be passed by Parliament, and that institution was preoccupied with many other matters. But Parliament would need to be persuaded to relinquish its control over the internal affairs of the Church so that clergy and lay people could themselves take on the responsibility of running their own church. 'Life and Liberty' was started by a small group of clergy who wished to generate enough support from within the Church to persuade the bishops, and the national government, of the need to enable this kind of change. And, many of the group believed, if this ultimately required disestablishment, so be it.

Temple, along with H. R. L. (Dick) Sheppard, was part of the group that drew up plans for the movement, and he became a keen member of its council (though he did not believe in disestablishment). The real challenge arose when the other members asked him to become its full-time worker. This would mean resigning the living at St James', leaving the career ladder of the Church, leaving the centrally placed rectory from which he had done so much, and taking on a temporary position that might cease after only a couple of years. He would also only receive one-third of the income he had been receiving. Furthermore, he had just married and his wife had just created a home for both of them in Piccadilly.

On the other hand, he was still searching for the role that would use his particular gifts to the full. He believed in the mission of the Church to the nation and in the need for the Church to reform itself if it was to carry out that mission. And he believed that the 'Life and Liberty' movement was the vehicle to achieve this. And so, at last, in November 1917, at the age of 36, he allowed the prophetic side of his nature to take the lead and draw him out of the safety and comfort of his current position into the bracing uncertainty of campaign leadership.

Henry Scott Holland wrote to Temple that 'you have gone over the top!' But he added, 'It does everybody good. God bless you!' Charles Gore approved. But Randall Davidson was less than enthusiastic. Such a move for someone like Temple was unorthodox, even freakish, and Davidson could not really sympathize with the passion behind 'Life and Liberty': why was there this need to reform the Church? And so the person who had been a watchful guardian over Temple's career, making sure that the son followed in the footsteps of the great father, now felt rebuffed. Temple, in other words, had finally made the break from his Lambeth upbringing.

The break came fully into the open when the bishops' Representative Church Council failed to take action on a report recommending the introduction of self-government for the Church. Temple and the council of 'Life and Liberty' were exasperated. The chaplains in the forces, who were in direct contact with the very people the Church was needing to win back, were almost in despair that the church authorities were not moving things forward. Temple, on behalf of the movement, wrote a letter of protest to the press saying that the delay to church reform was imposing 'a grievous strain on the loyalty of many who believe passionately in the Church, not as she now is, but as she has the power to become'. In ringing tones he continued:

> We are clear that the Church just now has her greatest and possibly her last opportunity of vindicating her Catholic and national character. But this can only be achieved by a struggle fierce and sustained, by a purging thorough and sincere, and by a summons such as many hoped might be issued during these days of war to dare anything, that the Will of God might be done, as in Heaven, so on earth. (Iremonger, 1948, pp. 244–6)

Davidson wrote back to Temple that his own difficulties in leading the Church were now 'greatly augmented' by Temple's letter, and that he felt it hindered the cause which he and Temple were both trying to advance. And he disagreed with Temple that the time was now right to push legislation for the Church through Parliament. The war effort was consuming all of the government's time and energy and it could not now think of church reform. The letter to the press could well stiffen 'convertible people into unconvertibleness'. The whole matter was a 'distress' to the Archbishop (Iremonger, 1948, pp. 247–8).

Temple was learning the cost of being a prophet. Davidson, as we have seen, represented a major part of Temple's own being, and to experience this division was distressing.

But his work for 'Life and Liberty' went ahead and he began in earnest at the start of 1918, continuing until June the following year. It involved travelling to different towns and cities, meeting with clergy and local civic and business leaders, mass meetings in the evenings, and personal talks and meetings of the 'Life and Liberty' council itself. Through all of it Temple spoke and argued for self-government for the Church. He urged everyone he met to join the movement so that the church leaders and especially the bishops would press for an Act of Parliament to bring it about. Temple threw himself into the work with his usual energy and enthusiasm and, in the first nine months of 1918, he had travelled to Manchester, Huddersfield, Great Yarmouth, Bradford, Walsall, Lichfield, Birmingham, Liverpool, Grimsby, Louth and Cambridge. He secured the support of vice chancellors, archdeacons, Nonconformist ministers, many parochial clergy, and C. P. Scott, the editor of the *Manchester Guardian*. In early 1919 he travelled to France and Belgium to secure the support of the troops stationed there. He also continued to edit *The Challenge*. And, last but not least, Temple led a delegation of 'Life and Liberty' members to meet with the two archbishops and urge them to support reform. The meeting itself involved 80 members of the movement facing the two archbishops in the dining room at Lambeth Palace. Davidson's ever-cautious manner meant that feelings began to run high among some members of the delegation and one member blurted out: 'The trouble with your Graces is, you're both Scotsmen.' Embarrassment swept through the room but Davidson remained unperturbed. He was, in fact, impressed by the strength of the delegation and at last came round to supporting the case for reform.[12]

The bishops' Representative Church Council now had to pass the various proposals before they could be sent to Parliament for incorporating in an 'Enabling' Act. It met in February 1919. There were arguments over whether women should be allowed to sit on the new Church Assembly that would administer the Church. The Dean of Westminster thought they should not. Temple argued that they should: were women not full members of the laity, and in many parishes were they not the mainstay of the devotional life of the Church? The advice of women on all the issues the assembly would consider was 'in the highest degree desirable'. In the vote the Council agreed with Temple.

The other issue concerned the church 'franchise'. Who was to be allowed to vote for representatives on the new Church Assembly? Should it just be 'communicants', or those who had been confirmed, or all the baptized? Gore and Lord Hugh Cecil and others were in favour of the confirmation franchise. Temple spoke in favour of the baptismal franchise: he argued (as ecumenical documents in the second half of the century would do) that all baptized persons were members of the Church, and that if they were excluded from voting they would feel excluded altogether from membership. The Council again agreed with Temple and accepted the principle of the baptismal franchise. Gore was upset and later resigned as Bishop of Oxford over this, among other issues. Temple in turn was grieved at this difference of opinion with his friend but, overall, was elated that the Church of England as a whole had agreed on a scheme for self-government. Davidson would now introduce an Enabling Bill to Parliament in the summer. By Christmas, with a little more campaigning from 'Life and Liberty' and some astute manoeuvring by Davidson, it had become an Act of Parliament.

What was Temple to do now? 'Life and Liberty' had been successful in its primary objective and the pressure was off. He had left his incumbency at St James' to devote himself to the work and now someone else was the rector. He was back with the old problem of needing to find a role. Various job offers had come his way, including the principalship of a church college in Agra in India, and the mastership of University College, Durham, but Davidson had stopped him going to Agra, arguing that his contacts with the Labour Movement (whose party he had joined in 1918), and the WEA, made it 'imperative' that he should stay in the home Church so that it should reap the benefits of his unique experience. The Durham job, he was advised, would involve him going to 'a small field' and both Gore and Davidson advised against it. The chaplaincy at his old college in Oxford, Balliol, was becoming vacant and Temple was tempted by that, though it would involve rather more academic study than he was now used to. Finally, a canonry at Westminster became vacant: this would allow Temple to continue to have a role and voice in the national Church, and this attracted him. What that role should be, though, was not so clear. He accepted the offer from the Prime Minister and wrote to his wife that Westminster would give

> what I think I most need after these three years of rushing about – and that is the opportunity and even duty to 'worship the Lord in the beauty of holiness'. I want (need) to renew depth in religious life, and the peace which goes with it, if I am to have anything to interpret to the world at all . . . Anyhow, I hope and believe this will [also] give us more time together in some degree of peace than Oxford would have done – at least in term. But there is a lot to pray about, and I had better begin. (Iremonger, 1948, p. 265)

While at Westminster, Temple continued to work for 'Life and Liberty', helping with the advocacy needed to get the Enabling Bill through Parliament. But his main work became the preaching duties of a canon, and the results are seen in a volume of published sermons, *Fellowship with God* (1920). Through many of the sermons Temple urges that the fundamental fact about human life is that God, in his love, has entered into fellowship with humanity through the incarnation, so that human life may, in answering love, enter into fellowship with him. The social dimension of this relationship, implicit in the word 'fellowship', was all-important for Temple and provides a connection with his developing views on society and the state. But Temple argues that this response is not to take place through the practical life alone, but 'in the perfect blend' of the practical life with the devotional life (Temple, 1920, p. vi). Up to now he had neglected the devotional life in his campaigning work with 'Life and Liberty'. At Westminster, he wistfully hoped to give more time to the devotional side of his own response to God.

But he was not allowed to remain at Westminster long. He was soon made an offer he could hardly refuse, and one which removed any agonizing choices and possible wrong decisions about which way to go. Sixteen months after arriving at the Abbey he received a letter from Lloyd George, the Prime Minister, asking him to become the next Bishop of Manchester. He was slightly dazed by the invitation and asked for time to think it over. He telephoned the Archbishop who told him to accept the offer immediately. Davidson, it later transpired, was behind the whole idea anyway. Gore told Temple simply to 'Go'. He wrote the following day accepting the Prime Minister's invitation.

So now, in the year he turned 40, Temple's wandering from post to post came to end. He would now live in one place and fulfil the duties of one (very demanding) job for more than a couple of years (he would be at Manchester for eight years). He would go north, to the second most populous diocese in the Church of England, and seek to lead its clergy and people in the work of Christ.

CHAPTER 3

Reforming the Church in Lancashire

William Temple had arrived. He was now a diocesan bishop, he was a significant force in national church affairs, and he was a respected writer and editor. He was now in a position to carry forward the passionate ambitions that had driven him forward to ordination in 1908, and he set about doing just that. His first ambition, a theological one, had been to restate the Christian faith in a way that was intellectually credible; his second ambition, a social reforming one, had arisen out of anger at the harsh social conditions of the time and was a determination to do something about them; his third ambition, an ecclesiastical one, was to help reform the Church of England so that it would practise the faith that it preached; finally, he had wished to convey to others the belief that Christ was not confined by human divisions but was the unifying Lord of all – an ecumenical ambition. Underlying all of these was his belief in a call to prophecy, to be like an Amos or Hosea who would bring the Church and nation back to God's justice and righteousness. During his years at Manchester, and when he was Archbishop of York in the 1930s, he had a vast range of interests and commitments, but these four concerns clearly and impressively emerge as the major themes of his work. Let us now take these themes and consider each of them in turn in the following four chapters. And let us keep in mind the question first broached in the Introduction: how far did Temple rise to the calling of being a prophet as he sought to fulfil each ambition? This question becomes more insistent as his ministry developed and grew before his premature death in 1944.

Dividing a diocese

The ecclesiastical theme can be the first one we examine, for the lion's share of his time in Lancashire as Bishop of Manchester was given over to church concerns and, in particular, with leading the clergy and people of his diocese. And here, if he was to fulfil his ambition of reforming the Church so that it practised the faith that it preached, he faced a daunting challenge. As things stood, it was impossible for the Bishop to care pastorally for the clergy and parishes of his diocese. It was huge, extending from the city of Manchester in the south to Lancaster in the north, and taking in Blackburn, Burnley, Preston and Blackpool. It included densely populated industrial conurbations, rural towns and villages, moorland and fells, and seaside resorts such as Morecambe and Blackpool. Above all, it had a population of $3\frac{1}{2}$ million and over 600 parishes (in 1847 the population had been 1.1 million). It had become too large for the diocesan bishop ever to visit all the parishes and get to know all the clergy. It needed dividing, as the Archbishop of York, Cosmo Gordon Lang, emphasized to Temple:

> There is the momentous question of the division of the Diocese which will require both great energy and great care, and you would have to put to the test your views about the division of dioceses which you expressed to the National Assembly [Temple had argued in favour of the division of the larger dioceses]. Further, it is only right to say that there are few places in England where Churchmanship and Conservatism go more closely together than Manchester, and I have long felt that there was need of some one who would make a more effective appeal to the new power of Labour than has been made in the past; but I am sure that this will have to be combined with some wise and tactful considerateness for traditions which go very deep into the life and history of the Church in Manchester. (Iremonger, 1948, p. 286)

The previous Bishop, Edmund Arbuthnott Knox, had epitomized both the conservatism and Protestantism of Anglicanism in Lancashire. There was a well-known saying that 'Lancashire is low', and the Oxford Movement, which had sought to spread Catholic thinking and practices within the Church of England, had made little impression in the county. Knox supported and reinforced this Protestantism. He opposed ritualism in worship and on one famous occasion, when he found a new wooden processional cross standing in the chancel at St Catherine's Church, Burnley, he took it down, broke it and threw it out into the churchyard![13] He also wrote *Sacrifice or Sacrament* (1914), a defence of the Protestant doctrine of the Lord's Supper against the Catholic influence of the Tractarian movement. He attacked the liberal school of biblical criticism and would later oppose the revision of the Book of Common Prayer in Parliament in 1928 and 1929. (His son, Ronald Knox, shared his father's opposition to liberal theology, as we have seen, but in 1917 was received into the Roman Catholic Church.)

Edmund Knox's conservatism was seen in his opposition to the dividing of the diocese and in his resistance to the pressure for division. He was an accomplished administrator who presided over every diocesan organization: he had imposed a regimentation that allowed the diocese to function as an institution under his own efficient administration. But his successors, if ever they lacked the same energy and enthusiasm for administration, would not be able to maintain it. And individual pastoral care of all the clergy and parishes had not been possible under such a regime.

Temple was different in every way. He was in favour of radical change to the structures and government of the Church; he was theologically liberal in his attempts to marry idealist philosophy with theology; he was of a central churchmanship that recoiled from definite extremes, whether Protestant or Catholic; in the political realm his opposition to the social conditions of the time made his radical sympathies stronger than ever: he had joined the Labour Party in 1918. And he was not enthusiastic about becoming a full-time administrator: he told his brother that after learning the ropes in Manchester he would only sit on certain committees and would not attempt to run them as Knox had done. And so when Lang had written to Temple that he would need some wise and tactful 'considerateness' it was, perhaps, an understatement.

Temple was consecrated Bishop in York Minster on 25 January 1921, and enthroned in Manchester Cathedral on 15 February. He was accompanied from Manchester town hall to the cathedral by the Lord Mayor and mayors of 30 boroughs. The judges of the Assize courts were also in the procession, together with their javelin-men! The suffragan bishops of Burnley and Whalley were also present, and in the ceremony in the cathedral the dean, on behalf of all the clergy, pledged 'loyal obedience and comradely support'. Temple replied by asking the people of the diocese to pray for him that he might 'never let go of the unseen hand of the Lord Jesus and may live in daily fellowship with Him. It is so that you will most of all help me to help you' (Iremonger, 1948, p. 291).

The first few months of his episcopacy, in his own words, were 'a wild kind of turmoil'. In the first six weeks he visited 24 churches 'with Confirmations apparently incessant'. But, 'it is jolly to be in a place where so much happens and one is really up against the things that matter. It is in that way far the most invigorating job that I have had' (Iremonger, 1948, p. 296).

The first task was to carry through the division of the diocese. The Manchester Diocesan Conference had already recommended that the diocese be divided. It had considered one or two different schemes for doing this, including the creation of two new dioceses, with one based on Lancaster and including the southerly part of Carlisle diocese, and the other on Preston or East Lancashire. After Temple had arrived it became known that Carlisle would *not* surrender part of its domain. The Conference then decided, in June 1922, on the simple division of Manchester diocese into two, with Blackburn as the new See town.

This was the first time that Blackburn had been mentioned in the debates. Up to this point the likely contenders had been Burnley, Lancaster and Preston. There was 'no little contention' in the diocese about the choice. Of all the towns, Preston was geographically the most central, it was the county town for the county council and one of the most ancient boroughs in England, but Blackburn was chosen. G. A. Williams, in *Viewed from the Water Tank*, a history of the diocese of Blackburn, thinks that the choice of Blackburn was due to the influence of Temple himself on the diocesan conference. Williams reconstructs Temple's thinking in the following, very plausible way:

The consideration which motivated William Temple was that Blackburn was not far removed from the centre of the new diocese, and there was a railway connecting it with the east and west areas of the county. The very large and predominantly Roman Catholic population of Preston was a further consideration. But the chief argument in Temple's mind was the suitability of Blackburn Parish Church to be the new cathedral. (Williams, 1993)

Williams then describes some of the reasons for its suitability:

It was a fairly large church, not yet a hundred years old, situated in a large churchyard which would allow for possible expansion. This same area of land about the church could also allow for the development of a Close in which the administrative offices of the diocese could be established. Furthermore, it was built on sloping terrain, being on the bank of the River Blakewater. In order to provide a level platform on which the church could be built, when it was erected in 1820–6, a spacious crypt had been provided underneath the church. It is quite probable that no future use of this area had been considered at the time of construction, but Temple could see all kinds of useful purposes to which it could be put. Again, it would be inevitable that the church would have to be extended if it were to fulfil its function as the mother church of a diocese which would be by no means small. Before this could be done, the platform on which the extensions were to be built would have first to be extended, and this would provide, beneath the church, an area in which there could be constructed a conference hall large enough to accommodate the Diocesan Conference, as well as a place where the members could eat, and other apartments to enable the cathedral to be an educational and social centre, as well as a home of the arts. From this point on Temple saw to it that no further consideration was given to any of the other aspirant towns to be the See town. Blackburn it was to be. (Williams, 1993, p. 51)

Not everyone agreed. Williams recounts how Lord Shuttleworth of Gawthorpe, who had served on Queen Victoria's Privy Council, thought the new diocese should be based at Lancaster, with the Priory Church as the cathedral. He thought that the county town should also be the See town. Temple had to go and drink tea with him and tell him that whatever he thought, Blackburn Parish Church was to be the new cathedral. From that day on, Lord Shuttleworth never mentioned Temple's name and gave up his patronage of the incumbency of Habergham (Williams, 1993, pp. 42–3).

It took two years from the Diocesan Conference for Parliament to pass the necessary Bill and for it to receive royal assent. The next challenge was financial. A Bishopric of Blackburn fund was set up to raise enough money to create the capital needed to pay a new bishop £3,000 a year and to buy a residence. Iremonger reports that £80,000 was needed and that Temple consulted widely about how to raise the money. He addressed many public meetings up and down the diocese, explaining what was happening and calling for support. A fund was launched at a meeting in Blackburn in 1925. A Mrs Elma Yerborough, daughter of the local brewer Daniel Thwaite, gave the first donation, a generous £3,000. Temple himself sold stock and made a donation of £1,000, but the richer lay people of the diocese were slow at first to come forward with other donations. At another launch the following year in Manchester, King George V, in his capacity as Duke of Lancaster, sent word that he would donate £105. Bishop Knox was present at the launch and now, generously, spoke in favour of the division. Other donations raised the total amount given to £24,700.[14] There was still a long way to go. It was decided that each deanery would be asked to raise £3,000, making a total of £62,000, and that literature be despatched to each church to encourage them in their efforts.

Many churches responded quickly and generously. Envelopes were printed so that people could donate even the smallest sums. By Easter 1926 it was discovered that the full £80,000 had been raised, with a third coming from the Deanery of Blackburn. Williams reports that it was a phenomenal achievement: 'No other diocese in the country had raised so much money with such rapidity for the creation of a new diocese' (1993, p. 54).

The Ecclesiastical Commissioners in London were now able to certify that enough money had been raised to house and pay the bishop, and so the new diocese could be legally created, with Blackburn Parish Church as its new cathedral. This was done by the issuing of an Order in Council on 12 November 1926, the date on which the diocese therefore came into being.

The final step was the appointment and enthronement of a new bishop. Percy Herbert, the Suffragan Bishop of Kingston in Southwark diocese, was appointed by the Prime Minister. Like Temple he had been educated at Rugby School, and then went to Trinity

College, Cambridge. For his curacy he returned to Rugby and then later became the incumbent of St George's, Camberwell. He was consecrated bishop at the age of 37, and moved to Blackburn at the age of 41. He was formally elected Bishop on 27 January 1927, and enthroned on 27 February by Temple and the Bishop of Liverpool. The new Bishop knocked on the cathedral door using a mallet whose stone head had been found in the bed of a stream at Whalley Abbey, and the shaft of the mallet was made from one of the oldest yew trees in the abbey churchyard. The *Blackburn Times* reported the event under the headline 'Flint Mallet Dints Church Door'.

The arrival of Bishop Herbert was the successful culmination of Temple's efforts over the previous few years to establish the new diocese. In what was meant to be an episcopally led Church, the Bishop could now, for the first time, in both Manchester and Blackburn, get to know all the clergy and visit all the parishes of his diocese over a four- or five-year period. The Bishop could become a pastorally caring shepherd of his flock. Temple had, then, gone some way to fulfilling one of his deep-held ambitions, of reforming the Church so that it could more meaningfully embody the truths it was called to preach.

Guiding a diocese

Reforming the structures was one thing: putting pastoral care of clergy and parishes into practice was another. Temple would only be able to be called a reforming bishop if he touched hearts and minds as well as structures. How well did he come to care for those committed to his charge?

The challenges were formidable. Even after the division he was still left with overseeing the second largest diocese in England. The work involved many mundane duties. There was the constant worry of finding enough funds to pay the clergy. By the time the diocese was divided he was able to ensure that every clergyman was paid at least £300 a year and that most were paid more than £400. The gap between the poorest and richest clergy was slowly narrowing, but there was still a huge difference between these sums and the £3,000 or more that bishops and some incumbents were paid.

Temple appointed suffragan bishops to assist with his ministry, choosing the name of Middleton for a new suffragan bishopric because of the ancient origins of its parish church. There was no area system for the bishops: they all roamed over all the diocese. Temple did not call his suffragans for regular meetings, though he did seek their advice on some matters. He made them chairmen of some of the diocesan councils or boards, but he never consulted them about parochial appointments.

He entered enthusiastically into the culture of church life in Lancashire, thoroughly enjoying the Whitsunday walks, when Sunday School children and adults would process through towns and cities, the girls wearing white and carrying baskets of flowers, the boys carrying an array of banners to the accompaniment of brass bands. He actively supported the missionary society rallies, as well as the Mothers' Union and Girls' Friendly Society.

He also instituted reforms in the way women were employed by church institutions, reforms that had been long overdue. And in 1925 the 'Form and Manner for the Making of Deaconesses' was used for the first time in the diocese, and a diocesan training house for deaconesses was established.[15] When he left the diocese the diocesan women workers wrote that he had 'done great service in raising the whole conception of the Ministry of Women throughout the Church in England' (Iremonger, 1948, p. 307).

Whalley Abbey, a great pre-Reformation abbey that had been dissolved by the Crown in 1573 and rebuilt as a squire's home after the Reformation, came on the market. Temple was determined that the Church should repossess it as a retreat centre, and appointed a committee to negotiate with the owner. The final price agreed was just under £18,000, which seemed excessive to some in the diocese. However, it soon became a valued house for retreats and conferences, and the diocese of Blackburn purchased it in 1928.

Money was tight for the Temples in Manchester. The previous bishop, Knox, received his pension of £1,700 a year out of Temple's income, which reduced it considerably. The bishop's house needed to be maintained and run, and there was little cash to spare. For nearly four years Temple did his travelling in trains and trams and only hired a taxi when it was absolutely necessary. A committee was finally set up to raise the funds for buying a car. The money was soon raised and Temple chose an Austin 12. He also set about learning to drive and became a painstaking, though never a good driver: he could only see clearly out of his left eye and complained that he had to 'look round his nose' in order to reverse. Nor could he claim any knowledge of what lay under the bonnet (p. 309).

One of the most memorable aspects of Temple's time at Manchester were the Blackpool missions. These had been started by Bishop Knox, who believed the Church should follow the people and who, on this principle, took a band of clergy missioners every year in the August Bank Holiday week to the town which had become a traditional holiday resort for thousands of Lancashire people. A number of platforms were set up on the beach, from South Shore to Fleetwood, and Knox called those he considered to be the best preachers in the diocese to address the holidaymakers on the beach. Knox had the habit of roaming round the platforms and listening to the closing words of an address. If the subject matter was not approved, the missioner ran the risk of being told his services were no longer required and that he could leave by the next train (Iremonger, 1948, p. 313).

Temple kept up the tradition of the bishop going to Blackpool. He decided to speak at midday in St John's Church during the week, with his subject, in the first year, being St John's Gospel and, in the second, Revelation. One of the other missioners described their apprehension when he learnt what Temple was planning to do:

Lunch-hour talks! In church! During August Bank Holiday week! In Blackpool! On The Revelation! Most of us felt that he was batting on a sticky wicket, and despite extensive postering not more than 40 or 50 people turned up. The next day there were over 200, and for the remaining days the church was packed, a queue outside stretching almost down to the Front, waiting to get in – a wonderful example of his judgment and an amazing testimony to his power of exposition! (Iremonger, 1948, p. 314)

The missioners stayed at Rossall School and would spend the evenings in each other's company in the senior common room, which was below the headmaster's study. It is said that Temple's roisterous and high-pitched laughter was able to penetrate the floor above 'where the headmaster would have liked to be busy'. Another missioner described how impressed they were with Temple:

His perfectly ordered and amazingly clever mind is a constant source of astonishment . . . At Rossall he is most friendly – just like a big brother to every man. His notoriously hearty laugh is a tonic, but all the time you feel he is reading you through and through, behind those veiled eyes. On Sunday night, after four crowded services, at each of which he had given a masterly address, I went into his room to find him busy editing the *Pilgrim* [a monthly journal on politics and religion]. He was still at it at eleven o'clock! In spite of the exceedingly strenuous week, he found time to read two volumes of French history and made notes of the same, and all this time he was suffering intense pain from a very bad attack of gout. (Iremonger, 1948, pp. 314–15)

Temple clearly enjoyed the weeks at Blackpool. During the one in 1925 he wrote to his wife:

It has been a delicious day from morning to night. I had an easy time, as I was only speaking twice this morning (Central Pier and Tower) and had no fixtures after lunch . . . I took a small and most delightful Confirmation at S. Stephen's – of the 5 dancing girls at the Winter Gardens, who are shortly going to New York. Then my address in S. John's . . .' (Iremonger, 1948, p. 317)

He also visited other northern parts of his diocese before it was divided. He wrote the following letter to his wife from Carnforth Vicarage:

Two delightful services yesterday – 13 [confirmation] candidates at Yealand and 63 at Warton (the mother parish of Carnforth), and 2 delightful Vicars. I shall have officiated in 8 churches in this Deanery, as well as 4 in Lancaster and one in Garstang, when I get home on Wednesday. I hope you are getting some peace and rest. I can hardly be said to be achieving that, but it is a rest in itself to be in the country; and a service in a country church is very refreshing. (Iremonger, 1948, p. 317)

Not everyone, though, warmed to Temple. According to Sir Walter Moberly, the Vice-Chancellor of Manchester University, Temple was found by some to be a little too impersonal and

intellectual for real warmth of intimacy, and his preaching sometimes went over the heads of the congregation he was addressing
(Iremonger, 1948, p. 318). Manchester did not, apparently, take
him to heart in quite the way Bishop Fraser, one of his predecessors, had been taken to heart. And so, despite his profound teaching
ministry, he would not, ultimately, be remembered at this stage of
his career as a people's bishop.

Temple, for his part, had one criticism of the people of Lancashire: 'Our people love to be doing things. They are a little
impatient of any effort from which they do not see some amount of
real result.' He was thinking especially of the business people of the
county and the way they combined great practical ability with a
sentimental kind of Christianity. He would have preferred them to
spend more time in thinking about and determining the right kind
of conduct, especially in their treatment of their workers, who in
many mills were still treated harshly (Iremonger, 1948, pp. 326–7).

He had, then, gone some way to reforming the Church, and the
successful division of the diocese was a significant achievement.
But there was more that needed to be done, and a different kind of
bishop would have made more of an impression on the laity of the
diocese. Temple was a good diocesan bishop and a significant
reformer of the structures he inherited, but he could not in the end
be described as a great pastoral bishop. His ministry did not significantly touch the hearts of the people he was leading, though it did
touch some of their minds, and especially the minds of the clergy.
His calling to be a prophet who renewed the Church found only
limited expression at Manchester. When, therefore, the invitation
came in July 1928 to become the next Archbishop of York and to be
freed from the burden of running a large and busy diocese, he had
no hesitation in accepting. He was enthroned as Archbishop of
York on 10 January 1929.

CHAPTER 4

Restating the Christian Faith

What of the first ambition he had described as an undergraduate, the theological task of analysing and presenting the Christian faith in terms of modern thought? During his time at Manchester and York he attempted to do this in a number of increasingly significant ways. The first was a modern restatement of Christian doctrine in *Christus Veritas* (1924). The second was his many lectures and addresses to student audiences, most notably in the 1931 Oxford Mission, published as *Christian Faith and Life* (1931). The third was a return to fundamental questions of philosophy and natural theology in the Gifford Lectures at Glasgow, which were published as *Nature, Man and God* (1934). And the fourth was an exposition of the fourth Gospel, to groups of clergy and laity at different times and in different places, an exposition that was as much a description of Temple's own faith in Christ as of the Gospel itself. The fruit of this work was his famous *Readings in St John's Gospel* (1939 and 1940).

Affirming the incarnation

Christus Veritas, his second major volume, began with the premise that Christ and the Christian faith were 'the truth' for all people, and it attempted to restate its main doctrines in the categories of the Idealist philosophy he had learnt at Oxford. Temple claimed the book was different from *Mens Creatrix,* which had been concerned with making a philosophical case for the underlying truths of Christianity. The second volume would be more theological in its

interests, looking at the nature of religious experience, the relationship between history and eternity, the nature of God, worship, the
atonement and the Trinity, and at the core of the book a meditation
on the significance and work of Christ.

Temple stated that the book was an expansion of a footnote that
appeared in *Mens Creatrix*. This footnote (Temple, 1917a, p. 318)
argued that the incarnation of God in the life, death and resurrection of Jesus of Nazareth perfectly represents, and fashions, the
entire course of world history, from the earliest beginnings at the
start of evolution through to the final stages of human history. The
incarnation influences the outcome of terrestrial history, in other
words, and it provides the key to unlocking the meaning both of the
world and of the peoples that live within it. His new book is a
'sketch' of how this is so or, in his own words, 'an exposition of the
Christian idea of God, life and the world, or, in other words, a
Christo-centric metaphysics' (Temple, 1924, p. ix).

How the incarnation represents and fashions terrestrial history is
shown in the course of the book. The presupposition, a very optimistic one, argued in *Mens Creatrix*, is that value, or as he preferred
to write, Value, is the ultimate reality in the world. The innate value
of anything one cares to name, whether it be an object or a person
or a situation or a group of things, provides the reason why it exists:
'Value is the element in real things which both causes them to be
and makes them what they are, and is thus fitly called Substance'
(Temple, 1924, p. 15). He believed, in other words, that everything
that existed expressed, to a greater or lesser extent, an element of
absolute value. Biological evolution and human history, then, were
viewed as part of one process, and this process had led to the emer-
gence of the supreme and absolute value which made sense of all
values. The world was an integrated whole, made up of a hierarchy
of being, with each level of being necessary for a higher level, until
the absolutes were reached. The goal of creation was the achievement of 'a commonwealth of values' – a human fellowship which
realized in community the values of truth, beauty and goodness,
inspired by absolute value.

He then argued that absolute value, which could also be
described as Love, was bound to enter into the process of reality to
bring about such a personal union with individuals, because that
was its very nature. It would want to enter into the deepest possible
fellowship with all those who had emerged from the evolutionary

process. It would need to become incarnate as a human being to call and invite all people into a personal fellowship with itself.

In this way Temple prepared the ground for his presentation of Christ. Christ was not just a human being but was absolute value, or Love itself, expressing itself in human terms. And he was a love who would sacrifice himself in order to bring about the final glorious realization of ultimate value, a value that was the crowning goal of evolution. Christ's life, death and resurrection was, then, the key to understanding the purpose and meaning of reality and, within that, of the terrestrial world.

In a key passage in *Christus Veritas* he summed up many of these claims:

> Christian experience is witness, not to a Man uniquely inspired, but to God living a human life. Now this is exactly the culmination of that stratification which is the structure of Reality; far therefore from being incredible, it is to be expected, it is antecedently probable. Even had there been no evil in the world to be overcome, no sin to be abolished and forgiven, still the Incarnation would be the natural inauguration of the final stage of evolution. In this sense the Incarnation is perfectly intelligible; that is to say, we can see that its occurrence is all of a piece with the scheme of Reality as traced elsewhere (Temple, 1924, p. 139)

Temple's christology was therefore full-blooded: 'We may say, then, without any hesitation that Christ is not a man exalted to perfect participation in the Divine Nature or Life; He is God, manifest under the conditions of humanity' (Temple, 1924, pp. 138–9). Taken as a whole, the book was an ambitious and impressive attempt to present the doctrine of the incarnation in the terms of Idealist philosophy.[16]

But was it a successful attempt? The argument, as already noted, was built upon the very optimistic premise that all aspects of reality could be explained by the value they contained and that this value could be seen to be progressively realized through evolution and history. But, as we saw with *Mens Creatrix* in Chapter 2, the fact and existence of evil in the world tends to undermine such optimism. Can Christ really be understood as perfectly representing the world when so much of that world is needlessly cruel, harsh and wasteful?

Temple himself had recently lived through one of the most destructive and pointless wars in history: was that also part of absolute value? The philosophical premise of his theology was becoming harder and harder to maintain and, towards the end of his life, as already hinted, Temple himself recognized that it would have to be revised. This, in turn, meant that ultimately his philosophical theology was open to serious question.

Christus Veritas, more than any other of his major books, bears out A. R. Vidler's comment that 'Temple was a theologian for Christmas rather than for Passiontide'.[17] As a book it gloriously affirmed the incarnation of Christ by placing it within the order and structure of worldly reality. But for those who found the world an irrational and disordered place, more like Calvary than the stable at Bethlehem, it did not provide much help. It did not show how Christ on the cross also offers a redemption out of this world. But Temple would himself come to see the need for that different kind of theology towards the end of his life.

Summing up the faith

Temple not only developed a reasoned theology but sought to present it to students and others in a clear and cogent way. He would speak every summer at the Student Christian Movement gathering at Swanwick. He would visit different universities and address their Christian societies. He travelled abroad and lectured in the United States on three different occasions, speaking to students as well as to teachers.

The most famous of these encounters was the Oxford Mission of 1931. F. R. Barry, who was the vicar of the university church, describes the background to the mission as being 'the disillusioned aftermath of the first war'. At Oxford

> religious and moral life was at a low ebb. College chapels were virtually empty. Christianity was almost a dirty word. Christian belief was commonly regarded as the refuge of the mentally second-rate – few, anyhow, were prepared to take it seriously. The job of the University Church, in that context, was to get Christianity back upon the map – to exhibit its relevance to the life of Oxford and as something intellectually respectable.' (Temple, 1931a, p. 11)

Temple spoke at the first mission to the university since the war. He spoke on eight consecutive nights in the church. He spoke without movements or mannerisms, with hands resting lightly on the lectern in front of him, standing motionless except for an occasional tilt of the head or the raising of a hand to adjust his glasses. He spoke of God's purpose for the world and how God had a purpose 'for us as part of His purpose for the world' (Temple, 1931a, p. 126). As was so often the case, he allowed a sense of the sweep of history, past, present and future, to inspire and motivate his audience to make a committed response. He spoke of the place of Christ within this history, and of Christian morality, sin, repentance, the cross, the Holy Spirit, prayer, the sacraments, and the Church. Through all of this he was able to present the Christian faith as a rational and coherent philosophy of life. And, apparently, he startled his hearers by his obvious and profound belief in aspects of Christianity which many of them had dismissed long ago. One of the undergraduates who was there, John Adam (now 92 years old and living in Lancashire) has written the following description:

> The church was packed with hundreds of undergraduates, thronging to hear him. He was large of stature and the picture of this great figure, high above us in the pulpit, is one I shall never forget. Unlike many missioners, Temple was not an emotional preacher. His powerful appeal was primarily to the head. It aimed to challenge, deepen and straighten our Christian thinking, belief and standards of life, and only then to stir our emotions. In all his eight addresses there was this element of challenge and every night, following the address, there was time for quiet reflection – silence, punctuated by quotations from Scripture, which helped to shape our prayers and our resolve. The silence ended with a prayer and a blessing and we all went out into the Oxford night stimulated, challenged and deepened, many of us with a new approach to faith and life. (From notes given to the author)

On the last night Temple spoke of the need for his hearers not to practise their faith in isolation but to bring themselves into the Christian society, the Church. In some famous words he described the history of the Church, a description which seemed also to sum up what Temple was doing at Oxford:

And, remember, the supreme wonder of the history of the Christian Church is that always in the moments when it has seemed most dead, out of its own body there has sprung up new life; so that in age after age it has renewed itself, and age after age by its renewal has carried the world forward into new stages of progress, as it will do for us in our day, if only we give ourselves in devotion to its Lord and take our place in its service. (Temple, 1931a, pp. 133–4)

It was all very inspiring for his audience. There was an unforgettable moment right at the end. When the hymn 'When I survey the wondrous cross' was being 'roared out' Temple stopped the singing and asked the students to read the words of the last verse to themselves. Then, if they meant them with all their heart, to sing them loudly; if they did not mean them at all, not to sing them; and if they meant them even a little and wanted to mean them more, to sing them very softly. There was silence while everyone read the words, and then a spontaneous and hushed whispering of 'Love so amazing, so divine, demands my soul, my life, my all' (Iremonger, 1948, p. 378).

Barry described how the mission touched and changed the lives of a large number of undergraduates, to the extent that many of them offered themselves for Christian service at home or overseas after leaving university. The mission 'was, indeed, a decisive moment in the history of that generation . . . It was when the tide began to come in' (Iremonger, 1948, p. 377). This is confirmed by Hastings who describes the mission as the first sign of a revival in Anglican Christian life after the scepticism of the 1920s (Hastings, 1987, p. 257). It seemed to be, as well, a moment when Temple's own gifts and calling came to be perfectly matched with the task he was given. He was, at last, beginning not only to describe an ideal to an unbelieving world, in this case the Christian life to the students of Oxford, but actually moving his hearers towards it. He was, in other words, beginning significantly to fulfil the theological ambition within his prophetic calling.

The text of his addresses also became very popular. It was reprinted sixteen times between 1931 and 1957 and reissued again in 1963 and 1994, the last time in an edition sponsored by Susan Howatch. *Christian Faith and Life* gives one of the best summaries of Temple's philosophical theology. It shows that despite the problems we identified in the previous section, his thought could still be powerfully persuasive.

Finding theology in philosophy

Did Temple become prophetic in other ways in the early 1930s? The question can be asked of his return to the borderlands of theology and philosophy in the Gifford Lectures delivered at Glasgow University at intervals between 1932 and 1934. The moment was good for him to deliver this prestigious series of lectures. He was now well established in his new role as Archbishop of York and he and his wife were happily settled in their new home at Bishopthorpe. He was freed from the time-consuming work of administering a large urban diocese. He had a certain amount of time for reading and writing, though apparently he was in the habit of writing out his next lecture on the train from York to Glasgow. He was aware that his previous essay on the philosophical foundations of theology, *Mens Creatrix,* had been written in disconnected moments of a busy life in London and had suffered as a result. He would have been keen to have another go at the pre-eminent intellectual concern of his life.

In the Preface to *Nature, Man and God,* Temple explains that his method is not to construct, stage by stage, a philosophical fabric where each conclusion becomes the basis of the next advance. Something more complex is being attempted: 'My own endeavour is rather to provide a coherent articulation of an experience which has found some measure of co-ordination through adherence to certain principles.' Later he explains what he means by drawing a comparison with the dialectical materialism of Marx, Engels and Lenin who, he recognizes, make a strong appeal to the minds of his contemporaries. He wishes to present a dialectic that has a greater range of apprehension and is more thorough in its appreciation of the interplay of factors in the real world than that of Marxism (Temple, 1934, pp. ix–x). In other words, the spiritual as well as the material dimension of life is included.

The method he was proposing can be explained by returning to the common root behind both Marxism and Temple's own Idealist philosophical background, namely Hegel's philosophy and especially his belief in historical development being fundamental to reality (sometimes called historicism). Hegel claimed to present a way of interpreting and unifying human experience and the reality behind it. He did this through positing the concept of 'Geist', a kind of controlling spirit of human culture, at work through human affairs and historical development. He saw the conflicts, struggles and resolutions of human history as the working out of an over-arching dialectical process, involving the three steps of thesis, antithesis and synthesis at every turn.

Marx and his disciples retained the grammar of Hegel's philosophy, as it were, while replacing the vocabulary. They continued to see an unfolding dialectical unity to history, but saw the controlling concept behind this as the struggle of the working classes for a class-free society. History was still seen as purposeful and progressive, but in a materialist rather than a spiritual way.

Temple also thought easily and naturally within the historicist grammar of Hegelian philosophy. His project was the attempt to update its Idealist vocabulary, as it were, with ideas and ways of thinking drawn from Christian belief, and to do so in a way which accounted for a greater range of human experience than Marxism. He was also seeking to improve on the outlook of A. N. Whitehead's *Process and Reality*, which he respected greatly. Temple agreed with many aspects of Whitehead's process thought but felt that at crucial points in the argument Whitehead did not sufficiently recognize the separation of the Divine Mind from the world.

The areas he included in his study of dialectical realism, as he now called it, were similar to those he discussed in *Mens Creatrix*. In the first half of *Nature, Man and God* he began with the fact of evolution as shown by science.[18] He sought to trace the scope and limits of human knowledge within this evolutionary process, and the likelihood of a unifying Mind lying behind the unfolding reality of the terrestrial world. He discussed the place of truth and beauty within this scheme, and the key significance of value as a concept which can explain why things are the way they are. He traced the place of freedom and determinism for individuals within the evolutionary process. Towards the end of the section he concluded that reality gives grounds for believing in a transcendent Mind or, as he now says, a personal Spirit, over and above the process of development.

In the second half of the book, he worked in the other direction. He began with the premise of a transcendent Mind at work through the whole cosmic process, and sought to trace the ways it is immanent within that process and can be known by finite minds. He discussed the nature of a particular revelation, which he famously defined as not being a set of propositions held as truths, but as the coincidence of divinely guided events with minds divinely illuminated to interpret those events (Temple, 1934, p. 312). He also discussed human finitude, the relationship of divine grace and human freedom, and eternal life. He optimistically argued that transcendent Mind can be seen in the way all values ultimately exhibit a commonwealth of value; and that human history also ultimately exhibits a dependence on eternity (though, in line with his historicism, Temple said that history is necessary and essential to the eternal, and that in an important sense it 'makes' eternity (Temple, 1934, pp. 448, 451).

Then, in a famous and brilliant aside, which was meant as a deliberate rebuff to Marxism, he presented Christianity as the religion that best expresses this materialist and spiritual understanding of reality:

> It may safely be said that one ground for the hope of Christianity that it may make good its claim to be the true faith lies in the fact that it is the most avowedly materialist of all the great religions. It affords an expectation that it may be able to control the material, precisely because it does not ignore it or deny it, but roundly asserts alike the reality of matter and its subordination. Its own most central saying is: 'The Word was made flesh,' where the last term was, no doubt, chosen because of its specially materialistic associations. By the very nature of its central doctrine Christianity is committed to a belief in the ultimate significance of the historical process, and in the reality of matter and its place in the divine scheme. (Temple, 1934, p. 478)

At the end of the book he summed up his view of reality with the powerful and evocative concept of the sacramental universe. He defined a sacrament as 'the spiritual utilisation of a material object whereby a spiritual result is effected' (Temple, 1934, p. 491). In other words, it is an instance where matter becomes an 'effectual expression' or 'symbolic instrument' of spirit: the spirit is first and last, with the matter as its vehicle. He then applied this idea to the whole of the created universe: 'the view of the universe which I have called sacramental asserts the supremacy and absolute freedom of

God; the reality of the physical world and its process as His creation; the vital significance of the material and temporal world to the eternal Spirit' (Temple, 1934, p. 493). But how is the world a sacrament of the Spirit?

> God, who is Spirit, is His eternal self in and through the historical process of creating a world and winning it to union with Himself. His creation is sacramental of Himself to His creatures; but in effectively fulfilling that function it becomes sacramental of Him to Himself – the means whereby He is eternally that which eternally He is. (Temple, 1934, p. 495)

In these passages it is clear that Idealist philosophy has given way to Temple's own religious faith as the controlling influence on his thought; and this illustrates an important comment on *Nature, Man and God* made by Emil Brunner in a letter to Temple. Brunner argued that Temple had failed properly to distinguish true, natural theology, which relies simply on logical argument and generally accepted facts, from Christian theology and dogmatics, which are regulated by Christian beliefs:

> So, for instance, your conception of religion is determined *a priori* by Christian faith, and is deduced from it; the same applies to your concepts of sin, love, personality, etc. This means, however, that in these passages your natural theology is natural only in appearance, whilst it is in truth Christian. In the third and final part of your book, your expositions are substantially, even predominantly, nothing more nor less than Christian dogmatics, even though the difference in method is repeatedly stressed. (Iremonger, 1948, pp. 531–2)

Temple had again mixed his philosophy with theology: on the one hand he had produced a book which was not impartial enough to makes its case to the sceptical (as well as the faithful); yet, on the other hand, he had not produced a book with enough exposition of the content of Christian belief to be of use as a systematic theology. *Nature, Man and God* could not convince the unbeliever of the truth of Christianity, but nor were its lengthy philosophical discussions aimed at helping the believer to gain a wider knowledge of the theology underlying the Christian faith.

Does that mean the whole book failed in its attempt to present philosophical foundations for Christian theology? Not entirely: the philosopher Dorothy Emmet, in an acute and sympathetic review of the book, states that Temple's philosophical writings stand as an impressive exposition of a reasonable faith (Iremonger, 1948, p. 535). In other words, Temple may not convince the sceptic but he certainly impresses the sceptic and makes him or her seriously engage with the issues of religion. Furthermore, Emmet suggests, some aspects of Temple's scheme could be carried forward even if his metaphysics ultimately fail. She quotes a letter that Temple wrote to her in 1942 and which shows Temple now thinking that the Gifford Lectures do not describe reality as it is, but reality as it will become in God's own time:

> The particular modification (in my thinking) to which I am feeling driven is not substantial, though I think it is very important. It is a much clearer perception of what is worked out in the Gifford Lectures about process and value. What we must completely get away from is the notion that the world as it now exists is a rational whole; we must think of its unity not by the analogy of a picture, of which all the parts exist at once, but by the analogy of a drama where, if it is good enough, the full meaning of the first scene only becomes apparent with the final curtain; and we are in the middle of this. Consequently the world as we see it is strictly unintelligible. We can only have faith that it will become intelligible when the divine purpose, which is the explanation of it, is accomplished . . .
>
> All this is really there in the Gifford Lectures, but I don't think the total presentation in that book or in *Christus Veritas* sufficiently gives this impression of a dynamic process and leaves too much that of a static system. (In Iremonger, 1948, pp. 537–8)

Temple still believed in a profound and unifying meaning within the universe, but now he saw that this would only become clear in the future (a position not unlike that of Teilhard de Chardin). *Nature, Man and God* could still contribute to this future-orientated view of the world, but only after some revision. Its argument would now have to be read as an extended description of the contours of such a hoped-for world, a world which would eventually produce a society of spirits united in a commonwealth of value. And the belief in the universe being sacramental would now have to be understood as a description of the universe not as it was but only, tantalisingly, as it would become. Temple's tireless and reasoned commitment to philosophy, then, a commitment which had sought to describe the world both as it was and as it was becoming, would now have to be directed only to the latter. But this, at least, would give it a more prophetic character: he would now be describing a new world, one that was growing out of the present world but was not always visible within it. His philosophy would now be explicitly based on faith and so, at heart, would become a philosophical theology. It had, of course, always been based in some degree on his own faith, but now he was clearly recognizing and working within that fact. He was, then, becoming overtly prophetic in his thought. In the next chapter the shift in Temple's thinking in the war years will be examined in more general terms and, with that, the increasingly prophetic character of his thought will become clearer still.

Meditating on the fourth Gospel

He had another weapon in his armoury, though, a more powerful one. He sought to restate the truth of the incarnation through an exposition of the fourth Gospel. He wrote that 'for as long as I can remember I have had more love for St John's Gospel than for any other book', and that 'with St John I am at home'. His exposition, which had begun to be formulated at St James', Piccadilly, was especially developed when he addressed clergy on retreat or laity at conferences and in services. He came to write the exposition down in the late 1930s 'in odd half hours', as he admitted, and it was published in two parts, the first in 1939 and the second in 1940, as *Readings in St John's Gospel.* It is not an exposition that drew on the New Testament scholarship of his time and so did not attempt to resolve any of the critical and exegetical questions surrounding the Gospel. It was deliberately a reading of the text as it stands and drew, for its inspiration, as much on Temple's own living experience of Christ as on the text itself. In his comments on one passage in the Gospel he gave a description of what the whole book was doing. Writing on John 1.14 he comments:

. . . as we read the story, though it all happened long ago, we apprehend present fact. It is not only the record of a historical episode that we read; it is the self-expression of that God 'in whom we live and move and have our being'; so that whatever finds expression there is true now, and the living Jesus who is 'the same yesterday and to-day and for ever' still deals with our souls as He dealt with those who had fellowship with Him when He *tabernacled among us*. Our reading of the Gospel story can be and should be an act of personal communion with the living Lord. (Temple, 1961 (1939–40), p. 14)

This is what the whole book presents. Through its exposition of the unfolding story of Christ's ministry, death and resurrection, and the dialogues that intersperse it, the book uncovers and describes not only the ways Christ related to his disciples but also the ways he relates to believers today. Using the text of the Gospel as a peg, Temple draws on his own and others' experience of Christ to present the living truth of the Christian gospel, which is Christ himself. In the introduction he describes his method of reading and writing in the following terms: 'I am chiefly concerned with what arises in my mind and spirit as I read; and I hope this is not totally different from saying that I am concerned with what the Holy Spirit says to me through the Gospel' (Temple, 1961 (1939–40), p. xiii).

While this kind of reading does not remove the need for philosophical theology, because on its own it does not convince the unbeliever, it does lead the believer far beyond the results of philosophical theology. Temple describes how this type of reading leads to a direct encounter with the truth itself, because that truth is a living person. Writing on John 14.6 and the words 'I am . . . the truth' he states:

Truth is the perfect correlation of mind and reality; and this is actualised in the Lord's Person. If the Gospel is true and God is, as the Bible declares, a Living God, the ultimate truth is not a system of propositions grasped by a perfect intelligence, but is a Personal Being apprehended in the only way in which persons are ever fully apprehended, that is, by love. (Temple, 1961 (1939–40), p. 223)

The use of the intelligence was not the way, ultimately, to know
God: such knowledge would come through a loving relationship,
taking as much time and involvement as any other kind of committed relationship. God in Christ would be known through ongoing
attentiveness to him:

> '*He that hath seen me hath seen the Father.*' Those are the words
> that we long to hear. We cannot fully grasp that supreme truth,
> as we should if our discipleship were perfect. We need to hear
> them over and over again, to let the sound of them constantly
> play upon our ears, the meaning of them perpetually occupy
> our minds, the call in them unceasingly move our wills . . . In
> adoration, in supplication, in dedication, let us take care
> always to address ourselves to God as He is seen in Jesus
> Christ. Never ask in prayer for any blessing till you are sure
> your mind is turned to Jesus Christ; then speak to God as you
> see Him there. (Temple, 1961 (1939–40), p. 225)

The truth of the incarnation, then, was to be grasped in the
same way that the disciples came to know Christ, through accom-
panying him through his life, death and resurrection. The
incarnation was to be known in its depths through the practice of
faith rather than in just the description of faith. The story within
the fourth Gospel, as it unfolds in Temple's hands, provides a
model of such practice.

Readings in St John's Gospel has proved to be Temple's most
enduring book. It was not his most popular book when it was published (that was to be *Christianity and Social Order*) but it is the only
one still in print 60 years after being published. It was a presentation of the Christian faith that made sense to a small but growing
number of people, and it has continued to make sense ever since,
even when some aspects of its style and presentation have become
dated. It was not a volume that set out to convince the sceptical of
the truth of Christianity, and nor did it, but it helped those who
wanted to believe, to believe with more confidence and assurance.
And so, surprisingly, it was this volume, rather than the more
rigorous and weighty *Christus Veritas* or *Nature, Man and God,* that
went furthest to fulfilling his early ambition of restating Christian
belief in a powerful and inspiring way for his contemporaries. In
other words, he most strongly restated the Christian faith not

through the strength of his philosophical arguments but, with the help of St John, through a description of his own living relationship with Christ. One important aspect of his prophetic vocation, then, was fulfilled in this quiet but profound way.

CHAPTER 5

Exposing
Social Injustice

As an undergraduate, Temple had been angered and upset by the social conditions in which the industrial population were living at that time. He had become committed to working for their reform and this had been one of the main reasons behind his decision to offer himself to the service of the Church. Through his contact and work with the WEA this concern had 'made' him as a person. Furthermore, as he moved from post to post within the Church he had continued with his work for the WEA even when there was intense pressure to concentrate on other things. In 1918 it had made him join the Labour Party which, he believed, presented the best hope for social reconstruction at the end of the First World War (though he resigned seven years later over the inconsistency of the Party's policy in the Far East, and also as a result of disappointment over its parliamentary achievements).[19] Now, in the 1920s, he remained as angered as ever over the lack of progress in improving social and educational provision for the industrial population:

> English civilisation is severely condemned. It tolerates gross inequalities in the educational facilities open to the various classes in society, and puts off the great majority with a mere introduction to education which stops short before true education begins. At this moment it is turning thousands of children out from its schools, not even into industrial employment, but into unemployment with all its concomitant degradations. And its industrial system pays scarcely any respect to the worker's personality at all. The deepest chal-

lenge presented by Labour to the existing system is the sense that it outrages the personality of the working man.[20]

As a bishop, at Manchester and then at York in the 1930s, he came to express his commitment to social reform in two main ways, which we will look at in turn. He developed and advocated his Christian social thought, which exposed social injustice as an affront to God's purposes for the world. And he took practical steps to bring about social reform, through organizing a huge interdenominational church conference in 1924, and through directly intervening in politics on a number of occasions.

A theory of history

Temple developed his thinking about society and the state in a number of articles and short books, the most famous of which was *Christianity and Social Order*, written while he was still at York. From the early 1920s onwards this social thought drew creatively from two main sources: his idealist philosophy and especially its view of the development of human history; and his Christian belief in the eternal loving Fatherhood of God and the ongoing sinfulness of human nature.

The idealist theory of human history arose out of a basic belief in the dynamic nature of the terrestrial world and the way it exhibited the unfolding purpose of Mind. Evolution, and within that, human history, was a process: things were not standing still and set in their ways, but were changing and evolving all the time. In other words, there was a belief in progress, though Hegel had shown how this was not a simple linear progress but was dialectical: one moment or movement in history would be contradicted by the one that followed it, but out of this contradiction a reconciling synthesis would emerge, and so the process would go on until a universal perfection was achieved.

In *Christus Veritas*, drawing on Plato as well as Idealism, Temple described how there were three primary relations in which human beings can stand to each other: they may ignore each other, compete with each other, or co-operate with each other. These types of relations are discoverable in all human relationships: 'The history of mankind – the story alike of individuals and nations – is the working out of these principles in their interaction on each other' (Temple, 1924, p. 81). For Temple, the history of states up to the present time had been mainly determined by the second relation, which meant that pride or self-interest had determined their relationships. Within civilized states, though, self-interest was not dominant: 'a deeper foundation resting on Reason grows beneath it' (Temple, 1924, p. 82). Temple optimistically believed that 'the course of progress as the growth of the dominion of reason can be traced in both the internal and external relations of communities' (Temple, 1924, p. 82). It could be seen in the rise of freedom within societies over the centuries, and out of that freedom a growing appreciation for knowledge, beauty and fellowship. He believed that Reason promotes unity and fellowship within the nation and that it would make nations want to share an equality with each other. Something like the League of Nations would be the natural outcome of this whole process. Then, summing up, Temple declared: 'That it is right to work deliberately for the achievement of that goal there can be no doubt, but in doing so we must take stock of our resources.'[21]

This theory of history accounts for some of the influence of Temple's social thought: it underpinned everything he said and it allowed his listeners to see how they could be caught up in the dynamic realization of a better world, a world which might seem far off but which was already being born all around them: 'For human History is nothing other than ourselves; and we make its meaning by living out its process in the power, already available to us, of the Eternal Life which is at once the source of that meaning and its culmination' (Temple, 1934, p. 451). It was an empowering theory which, as Dorothy Emmet attests, was able to inspire people's imagination and give them the confidence to go out and do something about the injustices they saw all around them (Iremonger, 1948, p. 537).

But Temple was not a blind optimist. He knew the coming of progress would not be easy. At this point his Christian belief in the persistent sinfulness of humanity influenced what he said: he warned that 'of any emancipation from selfishness itself, or any attainment of perfect fellowship in self-surrender to the absolute good, our historic progress hitherto gives no promise whatsoever' (Temple, 1924, p. 88). In *Christianity and Social Order* he linked this awareness with the Christian doctrine of original sin, describing how, from the time we open our eyes as babies, we see the world from our own perspective: 'each of us takes his place in the centre of his own world. But I am not the centre of the world, or the standard of reference between good and bad: I am not, and God is.' And only by the winning of one's whole devotion to Christ could one be saved from this inherent sinfulness (Temple, 1950 (1942), pp. 49–50).

Historical development would not, on its own, lead to the goals he believed in. Some other way was also needed, a way which would put people in touch now with true knowledge, beauty and fellowship. For Temple, this was the way of faith in Christ and trust in the eternal love of God: 'Man needs education; but still more he needs conversion. Man needs political progress and social reform; but still more he needs redemption; man needs peace and security, but still more he needs eternal life' (Temple, 1950 (1942), p. 88). And so any approach to social reform was going to need both aspects of this rallying call: the reform of the conditions in which people were living, but also the invitation to turn and stand in the saving light of eternity.

From theory to practice

Temple then took the step of deducing certain 'social principles' from his future-orientated philosophy and Christian beliefs. This he did for the first time in the journal *The Pilgrim* (reprinted in *Essays in Christian Politics*) and continued to do in the 1930s and, above all, in his famous *Christianity and Social Order* of 1942.[22] The social principles were a succinct distillation of his understanding of God's will for the future development of society, and they were open to being applied to a range of social questions.

The first he described as liberty, or the principle of respect for personality in all people. He explained that 'if each man and woman is a child of God, whom God loves and for whom Christ died, then there is in each a worth absolutely independent of all usefulness to society. The person is primary, not the society; the State exists for the citizen, not the citizen for the State.' This meant that society must be so organized that people can freely express their own personalities through deliberate choice. And that, in turn, meant that there must be 'the best possible training' so that people would know how to make deliberate choices: 'it is the responsible exercise of deliberate choice which most fully expresses personality and best deserves the great name of freedom' (Temple, 1950 (1942), p. 59).

Temple did not follow J. S. Mill, in other words, in believing that freedom was the simple absence of coercion. He believed that freedom depended on society and, in particular, the state fulfilling a positive role, especially through education, in equipping the person for a purposeful and creative life in which they would play their part in moving society forward. In the Henry Scott Holland Lectures at Liverpool in 1928, published as *Christianity and the State*, he reiterated and explained this positive view of the state's role in a person's life, though he was emphatic that the state had only a conditional authority and jurisdiction to do certain things: it could never be an ultimate object of political loyalty.[23]

The second social principle was an expression of the social dimension of freedom: 'No man is fitted for an isolated life; every one has needs which he cannot supply for himself; but he needs not only what his neighbours contribute to the equipment of his life but their actual selves as the complement of his own. Man is naturally and incurably social' (Temple, 1950 (1942), p. 62). This social fellowship is expressed through family life, school, college, trade union, professional association, city, county, nation, church. All these groupings need to be fostered by the state, which should give them the freedom they need to guide their own activities (provided the freedom of other associations is not injured). They are crucial because 'Liberty is actual in the various cultural and commercial and local associations that men form. In each of these a man can feel that he counts for something and that others depend on him as he on them' (Temple, 1950 (1942), p. 64).

The third social principle was also an extrapolation from what had already been said: 'The combination of Freedom and Fellowship as principles of social life issues in the obligation of Service' (Temple, 1950 (1942), p. 68). Temple was thinking here of both individuals and groups, that they were to seek not their own welfare first but the general welfare of all people. He described how we should use our wider loyalties to check the narrower:

> we can and should check these keener loyalties [to family, locality, business, Trade union . . .] by recognising the prior claim of the wider [humankind, nation]. So a man rightly does his best for the welfare of his own family, but must never serve

his family in ways that injure the nation. A man rightly does his best for his country, but must never serve his country in ways that injure mankind.' (Temple, 1950 (1942), p. 70)

This principle was the vaguest and most overtly Christian of the three, but it was consistent with the other two and showed their moral bearing. (In the 1920s he also included a fourth principle, self-sacrifice, but he came to recognize that this could only be adopted by those who had a deliberate Christian commitment and so he dropped it from *Christianity and Social Order*.)

It is significant that these three social principles do not include equality. Temple's schoolfriend and lifelong colleague R. H. Tawney became a passionate advocate of the principle of equality, understood as the demand that the gap between rich and poor should be narrowed and that all citizens should come to own comparable quantities of wealth. The state, Tawney believed, should undertake a re-distribution of wealth, through taxation and benefits, to bring this about. Temple shared much in common with Tawney, including a deep commitment to the improvement of educational opportunities for the working population. Temple was also, according to Tawney,

a natural equalitarian. He thought that the most important fact about human beings is that they are human – which meant to him the children of God – and that temper, while confirmed by his convictions, was in him so natural and instinctive, so obviously not an acquired attitude but a fountain of affection and geniality welling up from within, as to create in others the sense of brotherhood which it assumed.[24]

However, Temple did not agree with Tawney about equality. He believed that everyone had an equality of worth before God, as Tawney shows, but he did not see that this implied that everyone should occupy the same kind of position in society and be treated in the same kind of way. In his charge to the clergy of Manchester diocese he argued that

men are born with different capacities and different gifts, and if you insist upon the principle that everyone must be free to develop his own life [as Temple does], the result will be an emphasis on Liberty, but there will be no Equality; whereas if you begin with an insistence that all are to be counted alike, however different their gifts and powers, then of necessity you will put great restraint upon many of the citizens and possibly on all. (Temple, 1925a, p. 80)

The equality that he believed in, an ultimate equality of worth, was perfectly compatible with the idea that 'some should command and some should obey' (Temple, 1925a, p. 82). As far as the ordering of society was concerned, then, liberty rather than equality was to be the primary principle.[25] Temple and Tawney quietly but profoundly disagreed with each other on this key point.[26]

*   *   *

The three principles – of freedom, fellowship and service – were then applied to contemporary English society. We have already seen that when Temple looked at English society in the 1920s he found the state completely failing to fulfil its responsibilities. This was still the case in 1942 when he wrote *Christianity and Social Order.* He noted that the war had removed some of the unemployment but there was still much that was wrong: 'the problems were urgent enough before the war; the war has vastly increased their urgency.' In a clearly written and cogent chapter entitled 'The Task Before Us' he deduced, from the social principles, some important and radical conclusions about the future order of society. He urged Christians to call upon the Government to

set before itself the following objectives and pursue them as steadily and rapidly as opportunity permits:

1. Every child should find itself a member of a family housed with decency and dignity, so that it may grow up as a member of that basic community in a happy fellowship unspoilt by underfeeding or over-crowding, by dirty and drab surroundings or by mechanical monotony of environment.
2. Every child should have the opportunity of an education till years of maturity, so planned as to allow for his peculiar

aptitudes and make possible their full development. This education should throughout be inspired by faith in God and find its focus in worship.

3. Every citizen should be secure in possession of such income as will enable him to maintain a home and bring up children in such conditions as are described in paragraph 1 above.

4. Every citizen should have a voice in the conduct of the business or industry which is carried on by means of his labour, and the satisfaction of knowing that his labour is directed to the well-being of the community.

5. Every citizen should have sufficient daily leisure, with two days of rest in seven, and, if an employee, an annual holiday with pay, to enable him to enjoy a full personal life with such interests and activities as his tasks and talents may direct.

6. Every citizen should have assured liberty in the forms of freedom of worship, of speech, of assembly, and of association for special purposes. (Temple, 1950 (1942), p. 99)

These points are examples of 'middle axioms', which are broad practical objectives that show how abstract theory impinges on practical problems and issues. Temple used the term 'middle axiom' in his introduction to the Malvern Report of 1941, where he defined them as 'maxims for conduct which mediate between the fundamental principles and the tangle of particular problems' (p. vii). It was a term used at COPEC (see below), and brought to prominence by W. A. Visser't Hooft and J. H. Oldham in a preparatory book for the 1937 ecumenical Oxford Conference on 'Church, Community and State', and it became widely used after the war, being most recently advocated by Ronald H. Preston as a method for Christian social ethics.[27] Temple did not use the term in his own books but, in *Christianity and Social Order*, provided a significant example (especially in the above points) of the method it represented. He showed how it was possible to make useful connections between Christian theology and practical social and economic problems, through the drawing up of broad objectives, which different kinds of ethically motivated experts could then implement in their own fields.

In an Appendix, 'A Suggested Programme', Temple took one

further step. R. H. Tawney and J. M. Keynes read the manuscript of the whole book and, according to the Preface, made many suggestions. Temple also knew Sir William Beveridge who was about to publish his key report *Social Insurance and Allied Services*, the foundation of the post-war legislation that established the welfare state under the Labour government. Temple was clearly influenced by Beveridge and included in the Appendix some of the practical recommendations that Beveridge had been discussing. But, more importantly, they also followed naturally from the principles and 'middle axioms' he had described earlier in the book and they show Temple making a final connection between theory and practicalities. They included the following:

- decent housing should be built near where workers worked;
- family allowances should be paid to mothers for each child after the first two;
- wages should be sufficient for a family of four;
- milk and one good meal a day should be provided at school;
- education should be the primary occupation of everyone up to the age of 18;
- the state should eradicate unemployment through public works, as and when it arises;
- labour should be represented on the directorates through the unions;
- every citizen should have two days' rest in seven, and an annual holiday with pay.

To our ears these calls sound moderate and obvious: at the time they represented some profound changes to the way society was organized, but equally changes that a wide body of political opinion (Liberal, Labour and some Conservatives such as R. A. Butler) was calling for. Taken as a whole, these points show Temple advocating the establishment of the welfare state. While he did not coin the term, he was, significantly, the first person to use it in print, in his book *Citizen and Churchman* of 1941.[28] And he wrote, in an unpublished article now in Lambeth Palace Library, that if the state recognizes in every citizen something superior to itself, 'we get the conception of the "Welfare State", according to which the State exists for the sake of its citizens both collectively and individually'.[29]

But did Temple's social thought publicly expose social injustice and prompt social reform? Was it, in this sense, prophetic? At the intellectual level it was clearly successful in making a connection between the Christian faith, philosophical theology and the case for social reform. It shows the bridging role that Temple came to occupy, between the Idealist philosophy he learnt at Oxford, the theological doctrine he absorbed as a churchman and, on the other side, the social issues and concerns that were so pressing throughout his life. His life provides an example of the discipline of moving from practical issues and problems to philosophical and theological theory, and then back again, allowing the one to illuminate and guide the other. It provides an example of what is now termed 'practical theology' and found in many theological institutions in the British Isles. The social principles and 'middle axioms' provide an example of the action-orientated kind of theology that arises out of such dialogue. As an example of theological method, then, Temple's social thought was of enduring value, even if many of the specific proposals he advocated for British society have now been achieved.

But did his social thought make a difference? This is the question that must be answered if we are to see whether Temple actually fulfilled his early prophetic calling. The answer to this question is bound up with Temple's practical organizing and campaigning in the inter-war years, and we must look at that work before coming to an overall conclusion.

Mobilizing the churches

Temple's first major social reform initiative at Manchester was the organizing of the Conference on Christian Politics, Economics and Citizenship (COPEC) which met in Birmingham in April 1924. The idea behind it had been hatched in 1919 when Temple was at Westminster, and Gore had strongly encouraged it. The idea was to seek the will and purpose of God for men and women in every relationship of their lives – political, social, industrial, and the rest. Whereas previous conferences and reports had looked at individual issues and problems, no body had attempted an overview. The problems of industry were to be seen alongside the problems of education, housing and international relations, so that the whole field might be grasped. Four years were allowed for study and campaigning in all the denominations (including the Roman Catholic

Church, although they withdrew just before the conference). Twelve commissions were set up, 200,000 questionnaires were processed at 75 centres, and the whole of 1923 was spent in studying the replies and producing the reports. Twelve book-length reports were produced which, according to John Kent, 'summed up one side of the social thinking which had gone on in the English churches since the beginning of the nineteenth century, and nothing quite like them has been produced since' (Kent, 1992, p. 116). They proposed various resolutions, which the Conference slightly amended and passed. Temple became chairman of the movement and chaired the Conference itself, which had 1,400 delegates, 80 of whom came from outside the British Isles. When Temple opened the Conference he described two motivating forces behind the whole event: 'We represent here to-day the consequence of a spiritual movement in the Church prompted by loyalty and hope, and a spiritual movement in the world prompted by disillusion and despair . . . Our aim is to hear God speak' (Iremonger, 1948, p. 335).

The Conference passed smoothly, with Temple using his excellent chairing skills to keep the proceedings focused and purposeful. It ended with a general call

> on all Christian people to do all in their power to find and apply the remedy for recurrent unemployment, to press vigorously for the launching of efficient housing schemes, whether centrally or locally, and to secure an immediate extension of educational facilities, especially for the unemployed adolescents, whose case is perhaps the most deplorable of all the deplorable features of our social life today . . . we urge the immediate raising of the school leaving age to sixteen, and the diminution as rapidly as possible of the maximum size of classes.[30]

The Conference did not lead to a movement for change. This may have been because the final resolutions were too general and did not, for example, propose an actual scheme for tackling unemployment. Nor did the politicians of the day respond: the Labour government of Ramsay MacDonald was about to collapse and be replaced by the Tory government of Stanley Baldwin. Temple was unable to secure the support of Archbishop Davidson and thereby give the Conference an official standing in church life. Nevertheless it should not be dismissed out of hand: Adrian Hastings says of COPEC that its

> immediate consequences were small. Its importance lay within a longer process of adult education whereby the leadership, clerical and lay, of the Church was being weaned from high Tory attitudes to an acceptance of the Christian case for massive social reform and the development of a welfare state. In this it and its like were almost over-successful. (Hastings, 1987, p. 179)

This long-term success will become apparent as we proceed.

Intervening in politics

The lack of immediate political influence of Temple and those he represented in the churches is shown by the events of the miners' strike of 1926 and what came after. The background to the strike was the disorganization of the coal companies and that they were struggling to survive: the owners became determined both to reduce pay and lengthen the working day (even beyond the legal limit). The miners decided to strike because conditions of work were very harsh and pay was already barely lifting them out of poverty. Their slogan became 'Not a penny off the pay, not a minute on the day.' Only the government could resolve the dispute, but all it had proposed before the strike, in the Samuel Report, was a curb on the lengthening of the working day. No new money would be given, no national reorganization or nationalization of the industry would take place, no rise in miners' wages would be allowed. Neither party was willing to accept this, and hence the strike took place.

When the miners stopped work their action prompted the General Strike, a stopping of work by all the unionized workers in the country. The General Strike collapsed after ten days, however, and the miners had to continue with their strike on their own. It continued for six more months, although in the end they were driven back to work by starvation.

As the strike wore on, Temple joined a group formed by the Industrial Christian Fellowship that included Gore, other bishops and Nonconformist leaders, who decided to act as mediators between the miners and mine owners. They approached both parties. The miners were now willing to reconsider the Samuel Report, but the mine owners were not. The group then went to see the Prime Minister, Stanley Baldwin, to put the case for the government pushing through an adapted version of the Samuel proposals (substituting a bank loan for state subsidies to the mining industry). Temple reports that 'Baldwin was very nice personally, but not disposed to budge.' Temple saw that the government wished the churches would keep out of the whole business, for it believed that the churches were implicitly encouraging the miners to continue the strike.

What should the group convened by the churches do then? P. T. R. Kirk, the convenor, wanted the group to side with the miners in their push for the Samuel proposals. Temple and the others did not agree. He later explained that while

> the Church, acting for goodwill, may pass on technical proposals tending to promote [goodwill], it is quite another thing for the Church to take the field saying that some technical proposal (e.g. a loan) is certainly the righteous line of action. Cook [the miners' leader], of course, will call us rats if we do not fight; and perhaps will be right to do so: but we *must* stick to our own job. (Iremonger, 1948, p. 340)

Temple, then, was prepared to bring to light and expose a social injustice, in this case the plight of the miners, even to the extent of taking it to the highest levels of government and suggesting a certain course of action to overcome it. But at this stage of his career he was not prepared to take the next step of confronting that injustice and seeking to push for its reform. He and most of the others in his group backed down from any kind of fight.

Nevertheless, the intervention by the group has been heavily criticized from both sides. At the time there were many in the churches (including, it seems, Davidson[31]) as well as many outside who agreed with the government and thought the intervention needlessly prolonged the strike by raising the hopes of the miners that they had support from the churches. In other words, the economic realities facing the mining industry should have been allowed to take their course sooner rather than later: the miners should have been forced to accept a reduction in pay and a lengthening of the working day because there was no alternative. From the other side, the failure to side with the miners has been heavily criticized by more recent commentators, most notably Adrian Hastings. He writes: 'It would seem that this was the real moment of Church failure and that Temple, more than anyone, was responsible for it.' What should happen, Hastings asks rhetorically, when reconciliation is impossible because one party (the owners) are sitting on the backs of the other (the miners)?

> In some sense liberation [for the miners] has to come first, but to help with that can mean an at least temporary commitment to one side and to particular policies, not just general principles. If the churchmen were not willing to go so far because it was not their 'own job', then they could have better stayed out of the whole thing. (Hastings, 1987, p. 191)

Temple and the group therefore pleased no one with their intervention. And he later admitted that the group had not intervened in a very skilful way with the detail of the proposals, and that they had not known all the relevant information at the time they intervened.

However, within a longer-term perspective, a more positive assessment emerges. While at the time the group's intervention failed in its objectives, it did pioneer, in a real and public way, the kind of mediating role the churches came increasingly to play in twentieth-century British political life (most notably and successfully in the 1985 report *Faith in the City*). Temple's group became involved in the coal strike, and failed in that involvement, and paid a price. But they were seen, at least, to be trying to move things forward. Through their intervention the churches were taking important steps in growing into a role that had been initially pioneered by Cardinal Manning in the dockers' strike of 1889: no longer were the churches simply being part of the political and economic establishment of the day, but were becoming a positive critic or 'critical friend' of that establishment, committed to improving the lives of ordinary people. This was a role that would gradually be adopted with increasing effectiveness. Temple and the others in the churches group of 1926, to their credit, were in some ways leading the churches towards this new role in British society.

At this point in his career, Temple seemed to withdraw from

deliberate political intervention in social questions. It may have been because he had had his fingers burnt, or it may have been because he had also become heavily involved in the ecumenical movement. Furthermore, he was also drawn into the muddle over Parliament's rejection of a revised version of the Book of Common Prayer in 1928 and 1929. This took up a considerable amount of his time.

It was not until 1933 that he again became involved more overtly in the political process. This time it was unemployment that caught his attention. He was angry and distressed at the level and severity of unemployment in Britain, and above all upset that it prevented those affected from contributing to the life of their communities. He called together a group of academics and church people to investigate the issue thoroughly and scientifically. They managed to gain the financial backing of the Pilgrim Trust and began the research. At about the same time, Temple published a letter in *The Times* calling on fellow-Christians to write to their MP and ask that the *reversal* of recent cuts in benefit to the unemployed should take precedence in the forthcoming budget over tax cuts for the better off. Neville Chamberlain, the Chancellor, told Temple to stop inter-fering. Temple wrote back unapologetically, saying that he had every right to invite people to forgo a benefit to themselves in favour of helping the less fortunate. It was an ineffective plea as far as the government was concerned, but again, Temple was allowing a critical but positive Christian voice to be heard at Westminster.

Much more effective was the report itself, published as *Men Without Work* in 1938, a book of 450 pages. It drew on studies on unemployment in Blackburn, Deptford, Durham, Leicester, Liver-pool and the Rhondda. The enquiry looked at those who had been unemployed for over a year, and looked at the causes and symptoms of the problem. There were sample investigations of personal cases, and examination of the relief work already being provided for the unemployed. When the report was published, it was welcomed as a significant piece of scientific and human research. It reminded a wide body of people of the plight of the unemployed, and spurred both government and voluntary bodies to provide assistance in the setting up of no fewer than 1,500 occu-pational centres in areas of high unemployment, not least in South Wales. Temple's own standing as an informed and effective advocate of social justice rose considerably in government circles with the publication of the report. It was, perhaps, a sign of a more effective reforming role he might come to occupy.

Men Without Work, however, while leading to the better treatment of many who were already unemployed, could not and did not confront the underlying economic and social reasons that had produced the blight. It did not yet move society as a whole towards a more just social order. Temple's involvement in social reform, in other words, had not yet completed the circle from analysing society and understanding the need for reform, to pushing that reform through. He had patiently and impressively built up a philosophy of society, both as it was and as it was becoming; from this and from his theological convictions he formulated the social principles, which were an action-orientated distillation of his theoretical reflection. He had worked out many of the practical implications of the principles, seeing the need for radical reform of the social and educational structures of society. But it is probably true to say that, during the 1930s, he did not use his position to take the final step in this cycle, of organising and campaigning for the implementation of these reforms. He had exposed the social injustice endemic in his society: he had not yet really confronted and reformed it. He was clearly in the kind of position where he could do so: the fulfilling of his prophetic vocation depended on him actually doing so.

CHAPTER 6

Calling Churches Together

One of the convictions that had been part of Temple's call as an undergraduate had been belief in a Christ who was not confined by human divisions but was the Lord of all. The truth of Christ, he believed, was perceived not only in his own tradition but in other denominations and even other religions. Arising out of this he had felt called to use his ministry in the Church to help bring about a greater unity between denominations and faiths, so that the truth of the universal Christ could be more clearly seen in the world.

It was in the 1920s that he began to do something about these convictions in a serious and impressive way, and he did this through both words and actions. In his speeches and writings he developed and described a theology of Anglicanism which showed the natural place of and need for ecumenical commitment among its adherents. In his work as a bishop and archbishop he spent a lot of time calling together church leaders from other denominations and guiding discussion between them, discussion which led to the planning of what eventually became the World Council of Churches.

Teaching an ecumenical Anglicanism

One of Temple's most extended descriptions of his idea and vision of the Church of England was an address to the annual diocesan conference of all the Manchester clergy in 1925. These conferences were probably the most significant means by which Temple influenced the clergy of his diocese. He described what he understood to be the vocation and destiny of the Church to which they all belonged. Its vocation, he believed, was derived from its history. This history was of a Church that was heir to the continuous history of Christendom, and also heir to that 'new birth' which is called the Reformation. 'Both of these must be borne in mind, for both of them are equally essential to the constitution, doctrine, and work of the Church of England as it has constantly represented itself from the time of the Reformation onwards.'[32]

From the historic tradition of the undivided Church, he later argued, the Church of England had inherited its sacramental and especially eucharistic ministry: he believed that, technically, the eucharistic ministry of the non-Catholic churches was irregular. The Church of England had also inherited episcopacy, which was necessary to the preservation of the true Order of the Church.[33]

In the 1925 address as a whole, however, Temple emphasized the importance of the Reformation over what came before it. While the earlier reforming movement of the eleventh century is commended for its right intentions in recovering the spiritual character of the Church and its fidelity to the New Testament, it nevertheless 'did not go deep enough . . . it did not reach the roots'. Consequently, it was followed by a sharp decline which led to a 'decay which made the Reformation inevitable'. For Temple, the Reformation itself marked the recovery of two fundamental principles of Christian life: the supreme authority of scripture, and the duty of private judgement (or what Temple prefers to call the freedom of the individual religious life). Describing the first, Temple made a distinction between the authority of scripture and its interpretation: the interpretation of scripture, indeed, may vary both from person to person, and from one age to another. Scripture does not make any claim to describe the whole truth concerning God and his dealing with the world; but its supremacy remains nonetheless, for it is there, and there only, that we find God's teaching coming into its 'fullness' with the light blazing out in all its glory, in the Person of Jesus Christ (Temple, 1927, p. 197).

The other principle Temple described as the duty of everyone 'sincerely to make up his mind what it is that God says to him through the Scriptures'. But Temple did not see this as taking place by means of the individual alone. The believer will do it:

in the fellowship of his fellow-seekers in the Church; he will allow to the witness of the Church's authority, if he is wise, a weight which will override any mere whims of his own mind. He will never set anything which has that authority on one side merely because he himself 'can see no use in it' or anything of that kind, but he will recognise the duty of making up his own mind and of appropriating for himself, as far as the Holy Spirit enables him, the truth that is given to the world through the Scripture. (Temple, 1927, p. 198)

And so Temple's emphasis on the Reformation did not lead him to a narrow focus on scripture and the individual believer as the only sources of authority in the Church. He saw scripture as paramount, but scripture handed on by the life of the Church and handed on with its own authority, an authority worthy of respect. Ultimately the individual conscience could set aside the tradition of the Church, but only when there was good reason and when others in the fellowship supported that. Scripture and conscience were the ultimate sources of authority for him, but tradition had an important role to play as well.

For Temple, these principles were embodied in the Church of England. Its vocation and destiny was to live by them and in them: 'to offer the fullness of God's help to every soul but never to dictate to any soul precisely how that soul may best receive the benefit' (Temple, 1927, p. 202). The Church was to embody a freedom in its life that would be different from a strict and military discipline based on the fulfilling of clear-cut duties. It would be a freedom that would allow 'a fullness of individual apprehension and appropriation', by which he meant that it would really allow those within it to adopt and own the Christian faith for themselves.

And this vocation meant that the Church of England was in an excellent position to understand and appreciate both the traditional Catholic churches of East and West, and the Protestant churches of the Reformation. It was a vocation that would include reaching out to both traditions. Towards the end of his talk he described how as a Church

we hold out, as it is commonly said, a hand upon both sides to the other great Christian bodies. We can hold out a hand both to the ancient Churches of the East and to Rome on the one side, and to all those who with us are heirs of the Reformation on the other; and in that we have a position unique in Christendom, the full value of which can only be realised for the universal Church so far as we are true to both sides of our own tradition. (Temple, 1927, pp. 205–6)

Ecumenism, then, should have a natural place in the life of Anglicanism because this tradition was based itself on the living together of different traditions. Anglican church leaders would need to reach out, interact in dialogue and draw more closely together with the leaders of other churches because that was the inherent nature of Anglicanism. Ecumenical commitment, for Temple, was part and parcel of being an Anglican Christian.

Organizing for unity

In the late 1920s and 1930s Temple did just this, extending his hand to both the Catholic and Reformed traditions. His first encounter with the ecumenical movement had been as a steward at the Edinburgh Conference in 1910. This made him aware of the emerging movement among missionaries for the churches to work more closely together in the evangelization of the world. He was also involved with the ecumenical Student Christian Movement, having become involved when at Oxford and then becoming its most regular speaker at the annual Swanwick Conferences. Many of the student leaders of the SCM in the 1920s and 1930s were also inspired by Temple to work for unity among the churches, among them Lesslie Newbigin, Ambrose Reeves, Oliver Tomkins and Ronald Preston.

In 1928 he attended the Jerusalem Missionary Conference, which was a follow-up to the Edinburgh Conference and which brought together official denominational representatives, rather than just missionary societies. The Conference took place during the British protectorate of Palestine, and was accommodated in some military huts on the northern slopes of the Mount of Olives. Conditions were basic: there were no baths and no electricity. On one occasion the draught in Temple's hut was so strong that the candle he used to light the room would not burn properly on the table, and he reported to his wife that he had had to put it on the floor and write, lying on the boards on his tummy (Iremonger,

1948, p. 396). During the Conference he visited Tabgha and Caper-
naum and described Lake Galilee as 'most beautiful, and full of a
delicious peace. When the sunset light fell on the Eastern hills, the
steep sides were much greener than I had seen before, though the
rock comes through a great deal. The red in the Northern parts
became glorious . . .' (Iremonger, 1948, p. 394). Of Jerusalem itself
he wrote, 'I shall not forget the 20 minutes or so that I spent all
alone in Gethsemane, looking across at the dome in the Temple
area. It is the one thing that has given me "feelings" in Jerusalem'
(Iremonger, 1948, p. 397).

At the Jerusalem Conference Temple's ability to formulate concluding statements with every point of view woven into a coherent
whole was noticed and appreciated. He drafted the concluding
'Message' of the Conference, a statement which satisfied (he optimistically claimed) both the progressives and the conservatives.
As a whole, the Jerusalem Conference showed that, from now
on, there was a willingness in both the older and younger
churches to attempt to work together in missionary work around
the world.

★   ★   ★

But what of the way the denominations understood their own faith,
and the way they ordered their denominational life? The Faith and
Order Movement was created to bring the Protestant churches
together in discussion about these core theological matters, in
order that the churches might move more closely together. The first
significant Faith and Order Conference was at Lausanne in 1927,
with the second in Edinburgh in 1937. Temple was present at both.
At the first it was agreed that the Apostles' Creed and the Nicene
Creed expressed the faith of all the churches represented, and that
a future unity must rest on the basis of the historic episcopate.
Temple considered these achievements to have been very significant. In 1929 he was elected to be the chairman of the Faith and
Order continuation committee. Thereafter he never failed to attend
its annual meetings, mostly on the continent of Europe, and to
chair the executive committee, at which most of the important
preparatory work was done. At one of these meetings Temple
described to his wife how, at a lunch in a hotel in Denmark,

each person's plate was replenished from some other as soon
as his last mouthful of the last was off it. I got off lightly with
bits of smoked salmon, lobster, chicken and assorted vegeta-
bles – mercifully small portions of each. Then came a great
dish with several kinds of cheese and several sorts of salad.
There is a lovely instrument like a fish-slice with a bent down
flange in it which cuts shavings of cheese with delightful ease.
We got over knotty points in the Agenda until tea-time.
(Iremonger, 1948, pp. 403–4)

Temple's considerable skill in guiding discussion and producing
comprehensive statements at the end resulted in his then being
elected the chairman at the world Faith and Order Conference in
Edinburgh in 1937. This Conference passed a final 'affirmation'
that seems to bear Temple's theological stamp:

We are divided in the outward forms of our life in Christ,
because we understand differently His will for His Church.
We believe, however, that a deeper understanding will lead us
towards a united apprehension of the truth as it is in Jesus. We
humbly acknowledge that our divisions are contrary to the
will of Christ and we pray God in His mercy to shorten the
days of our separation and to guide us by His Spirit into
fullness of unity. (Iremonger, 1948, pp. 426–7)

This statement does not pretend that differences do not exist
between the churches, and does not try to ignore them. But it
places great store in the power of dialogue and agreement between
the churches, so that such differences could be overcome in time
and that a full unity could come about. This placing of hope in the
power of reasonableness and in what the future could bring is very
characteristic of Temple, and it has become characteristic of the
whole Faith and Order movement in the twentieth century. It
shows how his leadership was so well matched to the ecumenical
needs of the time.

*   *   *

During the 1930s, Temple played a key role in the development of the idea for a world council of churches. He worked closely with two significant figures in the international ecumenical movement: J. H. Oldham, a slightly deaf Free Church of Scotland secretary of the International Missionary Council, who later became chairman of research in the Life and Work arm of the ecumenical movement; and William Paton, an English Presbyterian who had been a missionary in India and was Oldham's forceful successor at the International Missionary Council. Oldham, Paton and Temple have been described as 'the ecclesiastical statesmen of Protestant Europe, dexterously creating the structures for the Church of the future' (Hastings, 1987, p. 302). Of the three it was Temple who became the public representative. Their work resulted in the most enduring ecclesiastical development of the 1930s.

The idea of a world council of churches was developed during an informal meeting at Bishopthorpe in May 1933, at which ten people representing different international ecumenical bodies talked together and developed a new sense of shared leadership. At another informal meeting at Princeton in 1935, Temple took the lead in proposing an 'interdenominational, international council representing all the churches'. Then in July 1937 he chaired the so-called Committee of Thirty-Five meeting at Westfield College, London, which formulated the precise proposal for a 'World Council of Churches'. This was subsequently accepted by the international ecumenical 'Life and Work' Conference at Oxford (chaired by Bishop Bell of Chichester) and by the Edinburgh Conference that summer. The next year at Utrecht, Temple was elected chairman of the provisional World Council's central committee, with Wim Visser't Hooft, Oldham's assistant, as one of two general secretaries, and Paton as the other.

As Archbishop of York he was the most senior church leader to be involved in these discussions, and this partly explains his rise to leadership of the movement. But his rise was also due to his considerable skills as an advocate of the idea and, underlying all, to his own theology of the Church which, as we have seen, was one that accepted other churches as fellow pilgrims along the way. Adrian Hastings writes that 'It is unlikely that the World Council would have been proposed, agreed to, and brought into existence without his combination of authority and persuasiveness.'[34] If Temple had lived he would almost certainly have become the first president of the World Council of Churches when it was formally constituted in 1948.

*   *   *

The Roman Catholic Church, which was not part of any of these discussions, was also approached by Temple. In February 1939 he wrote to the Cardinal Secretary of State at the Vatican informing him of the plans to establish the WCC and expressing the hope that it might be possible to exchange information on matters of common interest, and that the WCC 'should have the help from time to time of unofficial consultation with Roman Catholic theologians and scholars'. Several months passed before an answer was received, but the answer was that the cardinal saw no obstacles in the way of carrying out Temple's proposals (Iremonger, 1948, p. 412). Temple's hand of friendship had not been rebuffed: it was a small but significant bridgehead across an immense ecumenical divide.

Temple also began to work with the Roman Catholic leader in England and Wales, Cardinal Hinsley. They shared a platform in the Albert Hall with the Chief Rabbi and Herbert Morrison at the end of 1938 calling for a national response to the persecution of the Jews. Then, after the outbreak of war, Temple and Hinsley, who now shared a friendship and respected each other, signed a joint letter with other religious leaders to *The Times* supporting the Pope's five peace points as the only sure foundation for European peace. It was clear the ecumenical fraternity was now being widened to include the Roman Catholic Church in England. Finally, Temple, who in his thirties had claimed to be the only English clergyman who had read St Thomas Aquinas' *Summa Theologiae* from end to end, addressed an audience of English Dominicans at the London Aquinas Society in October 1943 on 'Thomism and Modern Needs'. His address was a sympathetic appreciation of all that the father of modern Roman Catholic theology could give to the producing of a new 'map of the world'. A former president of the society wrote that Temple's words reflected 'the prevailing spirit of collaboration among Christians and of co-operation in all charity'. When Temple died, Hinsley's successor, Archbishop Griffin, described how, with the talk, Temple was 'breaking new ground with his eager and adventurous mind and that warm charity which drew new friends to him all through his life' (Iremonger, 1948, p. 421).

★   ★   ★

At the same time as the plans were being laid for the WCC, the churches in the British Isles were also reaching agreement, after protracted discussions, on the establishment of a British Council of Churches (but without the Roman Catholics). Temple was part of these discussions and supported the plans. In 1940 he had proposed a resolution to the Church Assembly of the Church of England welcoming the establishment of the World Council and paving the way for its counterpart in the British Isles, and this had been passed. Then at the climax of this process, in September 1942, he preached at the service of the inauguration of the BCC in St Paul's Cathedral. His sermon explained why it was so important that the different churches, which had distinctive principles and commitments, should nevertheless come together in a body like the British Council of Churches:

> in days like these, when the basic principles of Christianity are widely challenged and in many quarters expressly repudiated, the primary need is for clear and united testimony to Christianity itself. The difference between Catholic and Protestant is very small as compared with the difference between Christian and non-Christian, between those who do and those who do not believe that in Jesus Christ God 'hath visited and redeemed his people'.
>
> Our differences remain: we shall not pretend that they are already resolved into unity or harmony. But we take our stand on the common faith of Christendom, faith in God, Creator, Redeemer, and Sanctifier; and so standing together we invite [all] to share that faith and call on all to conform their lives to the principles derived from it. (Iremonger, 1948, p. 414)

The sermon was an impressive culmination of all his efforts, national and international, to call the churches together over the previous fifteen years. The work showed that in this respect he was not just someone who talked about a future Christian unity in a theoretical way, but gave equal attention to the practical business of convening, chairing and implementing the process of bringing it about.

In general it is clear that Temple was not responsible for pioneering the ecumenical movement: the delegates at the Edinburgh Conference in 1910 were probably responsible for that. He was not, then, a herald or prophet of the ecumenical ideal. But he was responsible, along with Oldham and Paton, for decisively moving the Protestant churches towards an enduring structural expression of it: he and they became its instruments. Of the three, furthermore, he was the only one to truly straddle Faith and Order (from the Lausanne Conference onwards), the international missionary movement (from the Jerusalem Conference onwards), and the Life and Work arm (through his drafting of the final 'Message' of the Oxford Conference of 1937). Looking back on the development of the movement, Visser't Hooft commented that 'William Temple had a unique place in the ecumenical movement. He belonged to all parts of it.'[35]

While his achievements did not stop the churches being divided from one another (in some ways the divisions became more intractable during the war years, as John Kent shows[36]), they did show that the churches had begun to work together. It was a start and, in the light of previous bitter divisions between the churches, it can be seen as breathtaking in its audacity.

Offering theological leadership

Over the course of the 1930s, unexpectedly and impressively, Temple shifted his whole theological stance. The rise of the Nazis, together with the division in the German Protestant churches over what attitude to adopt towards them, created confusion and uncertainty in the whole European and British theological community. As a senior churchman, in contact with national affairs and with international theologians through the ecumenical movement, he was profoundly affected.

To trace this shift we should start with Temple's chairmanship of the Archbishops' Doctrine Commission. This had been appointed by Archbishop Davidson in 1922 to bring to expression the core elements of Christian doctrine upon which all wings of the Church of England were agreed. Twenty-five people were appointed to the commission, broadly representing the Protestant, Catholic and

Liberal traditions within the Church. Temple was appointed chairman in 1925 and called the group together annually, with small working parties meeting twice annually. It was a long-term process, for the report was not finally published until 1938. When the report was published, the world was very different from how it had been in 1922. Temple acknowledged this in his chairman's introduction, where he described great changes in secular science, philosophy, political thought and theology, where 'the work of such writers as Karl Barth in Europe and Reinhold Niebuhr in America has set many problems in a new perspective' (p. 6). But while in its sections on the Church and the sacraments, the report showed the influence of Catholic thought on the mainstream of Anglicanism and the way in which the old divisions between traditions were beginning to be broken down, as a whole it was a self-confessedly pondered and rather dull document. Given the times in which the commission was meeting, it was remarkable for what it did not say more than for what it did. The Church of England, in an official capacity, at this late stage in the unfolding European tragedy of the 1930s, showed itself unwilling or unable to respond theologically to what was happening all around it.

But Temple, in his introduction to the report, did respond in a significant way. He suggested that there now needed to be a shift of emphasis, from a theology of incarnation (which had been characteristic of the last 50 years in Anglican thought) to a theology of redemption. By 'theology of the incarnation' he meant the kind of outlook that looked for the presence and work of Christ in the world as it currently stood, and believed that all that was necessary was to open our eyes and trace his presence all around. But a theology of redemption 'tends rather to sound the prophetic note; it is more ready to admit that much in this evil world is irrational and strictly unintelligible; and it looks to the coming of the Kingdom as a necessary preliminary to the full comprehension of much that now is'. So, 'If the security of the nineteenth century, already shattered in Europe, finally crumbles away in our own country, we shall be pressed more and more towards a theology of Redemption' (p. 17).

In a letter to Dom Gregory Dix in 1939 he described how his own early writings had fallen into the 'incarnational' category and were now unable to address the world of the 1930s:

So far as [my work in the field of theology] has had an influence, I think it was due to the fact that I was a philosopher, by profession at least, before I seriously turned to theology, and I was able to build bridges across which people could travel, from the outlook common in universities and such places from 1910 to 1920 or even 1930, to a Christo-centric view of the world. That is what *Mens Creatrix* and *Christus Veritas* are all about. I don't think it was a blind alley, because I do think it led to Christ. The trouble with it now is not where it leads to, but where it starts from; and this is a point at which nowadays an increasing number do not stand, though some still do. (Iremonger, 1948, p. 606)

As war approached, a different starting-point became necessary. In A. R. Vidler's terms, Temple now recognized that he had been a theologian for Christmas rather than for Passiontide, but now there was a need for a theology of the Passion.[37] In the introduction to the doctrine report he suggested that if the commission began its work again it should concentrate on the themes of redemption, justification and conversion. And the Church as a whole should turn from an emphasis on the pastoral ministry alone to one which is 'as much evangelistic as pastoral'.

These thoughts were then developed in one of the most revealing pieces Temple ever wrote, an article in the journal *Theology* simply entitled 'Theology To-day'. It was written as a response to a growing rift between the theologians of his own generation and younger theologians such as E. L. Mascall, V. A. Demant and Dom Gregory Dix. The latter rejected the whole attempt to marry theology with idealist philosophy, and were wanting to base a new Anglican theology on the neo-Thomism of continental philosophical theologians like Jacques Maritain. In the article, Temple looked back on his own theological journey, recalling his debt to the idealist philosophy of Edward Caird, Bernard Bosanquet and Josiah Royce. He recognized that now something else was needed. He quoted his own statement in *Christus Veritas* that what was needed was a 'christo-centric' metaphysics and now stated that this would not be a practicable task in anything less than many generations. With humility, he wrote,

our task with this world is not to explain it but to convert it. Its
needs can be met, not by the discovery of its own immanent
principle in signal manifestation through Jesus Christ, but
only by the shattering impact upon its self-sufficiency and
arrogance of the Son of God crucified, risen and ascended,
pouring forth that explosive and disruptive energy which is
the Holy Ghost. He is the source of fellowship and all true fellowship comes from Him. But in order to fashion true
fellowship in such a world as this, and out of such men and
women as we are, He must first break up sham fellowships
with which we have been deluding ourselves. (Temple, 1940a,
pp. 101–2)

The whole tone of this statement is quite different from his earlier
writings. It is speaking of a divine judgement upon the current
order of things in a way which Temple never used to do. It shows the
influence of Niebuhr, whom Temple knew and respected, as well as
possibly Barth (though Temple denied any direct influence).[38] It
shows the development of a more overtly prophetic standpoint,
with the way to the future now seen as lying through a cleansing
break-up of the ways of the world. We should, however, also note
the continuities with Temple's earlier thought: there is still an overriding concern with the coming of a better future, though now he
sees it coming in a different way. And there is still a concern with
the social nature of that future, being one of fellowship, though now
this fellowship is seen not to come through human progress but
through God's intervention in history.

Temple next considered his treatment of the problem of evil in
his earlier books, a treatment which we found to be problematic.
He now believed that 'formally' it covered the ground but, again
with humility, he recognized that, to the new generation of theologians, the approach, the tone, the emphasis, all seemed to be
wrong:

War – nothing less – overshadows life. We have to maintain
our faith in God under the shadow and shock of war. Facile
generalisations are an affront. We must start from the fearful
tension between the doctrine of the Love of God and the
actual facts of daily experience. When we have eliminated war,
it will be time to discuss whether its monstrous evil can then

be seen as a 'constituent element of the absolute good' (*Christus Veritas*, p. 254). Till then we had better get on with the job of eliminating it by the power of the Gospel, which we must present, not as the clue to a universal synthesis, but as the source of world-transformation. (Temple, 1940a, p. 103)

These are deeply impressive statements for someone who could have easily rested on his laurels and not questioned his three major works of philosophical theology. But now he was prepared to acknowledge that his treatment of the problem of evil was inadequate and, with that, to question the foundations of his christocentric metaphysics. He now recognized that evil could not be justified in the current order of things. And he believed that propping up his own theological reputation was less important than bridging the increasing divide in the theological community.

But, again, continuity must also be noted. The overriding concern, here as before, was the future and especially with moving the world towards God's new world. So, with this in view, Temple saw two main tasks for theological reflection. The first was the 'thinking out afresh what are the standards of life to which a society must aim at conforming if it is to be in any sense a Christian society' (Temple, 1940a, p. 104). This was an ethical and social question, and it showed how theology was called to be practical, to offer guidance on the problems of daily living. The second task was to 'recover our apprehension of the Gospel', a gospel of redemption, 'a deliverance from the system of things – "the world" – which deserves the destruction which is coming upon it . . . We proclaim, not general progress, but salvation to them that believe' (Temple, 1940a, p. 106). Temple ended his article with the call to dig the foundations deeper than before, and 'to light beacons in the darkness rather than to illuminate the world' (Temple, 1940a, p. 107).

To encourage this to happen within the Church of England he called a number of meetings with the younger theologians, not only with the neo-Thomists but also with others who had been influenced by Karl Barth's rejection of natural theology and his construction of a dogmatic theology based on revelation. There were two meetings in 1940 and one in 1944. The younger and the older groups did not agree on fundamentals, and when the scheme to unite the churches of South India was dividing those of Catholic tradition from the rest, the divisions became altogether more fraught. But Temple was greatly stimulated by the discussion and debate and allowed the new ideas to influence and form his own thinking. The others came away impressed, above all, by what one of them described as 'the fact of his holiness' (Iremonger, 1948, p. 610.)

He incorporated some of this new theology in his own writings on a number of occasions, notably in February 1944 in 'What Christians stand for in the Secular World', a supplement to the *Christian News Letter.* Here, in memorable words, he wrote that Christianity still

> enables us to 'make sense' of the world, not meaning that we can show that it is sense, but with the more literal and radical meaning of making into sense what, till it is transformed, is largely nonsense – a disordered chaos waiting to be reduced to order as the Spirit of God gives it shape. (Temple, 1958, pp. 243–4)

Through all of this, Temple was, perhaps, rediscovering the vocation that had come to him as an undergraduate. At the age of 20 and 21 he had heard the call to become a prophet of a new world, both for society and the Church, and it had been a deep and powerful call within him. At notable moments in his life this vocation had found clear expression, as when he had given himself entirely to the 'Life and Liberty' movement, or when he had sought to intervene in the coal strike of 1926. At other times it had been present in less prominent ways when he had become engrossed in administering the structures of the Church. But a commitment to presenting the ideal of God's new world, and moving society towards it through the Church, was the connecting thread that ran through all his work. And now, as the Second World War began, this prophetic vocation began to reassert itself. He saw that proclaiming God's new world also entailed words of judgement on the past and present, not least on his own work as a philosophical theologian; and he saw that it also entailed working out the practical implications for ethics and for the ordering of society, and then of doing something about putting them into practice. It was no longer enough just talking about 'the hope of a new world' (which became the title of a 1940 collection of Temple's sermons), but of moving society as a whole towards it.

By the time he was enthroned as Archbishop of Canterbury in April 1942, Temple had therefore arrived at a point in his life where he had not only become a leader of the Christian community in England, and (as we shall see) had become a recognized leader of the British people as a whole, but he had also rediscovered his calling to prophecy. His theological reflection at the outset of the war, stimulated by discussion with others, had brought him to this point. He saw that the Church, and within the Church voices such as his own, were now called to proclaim both a word of judgement on the current chaotic order of things, and a word of encouragement to all people to take up the social and ethical task of conforming this world to God's forthcoming new world.

The question that remained was this: was Temple going to take that final step himself? He had talked and written about the need to be prophetic; he had the authority and position to be heard as a prophet; was he now going to actually become prophetic to the society in which he lived? Was he going to throw himself into the task not only of presenting God's judging and redeeming new world, but of somehow moving the old world closer towards it? Was he, in other words, going to take one final step in the fulfilment of his prophetic calling, the step of decisively prophesying to the nation?

CHAPTER 7

Speaking to the Nation

Facing war in Europe

The 1930s were a time of increasing disarray in British politics. The rise of Nazism in Germany and Fascism in Italy, with their attendant horrors, came to change the whole political landscape. After the economic turmoil of the Great Crash in 1929 and the need for strong national leadership, especially in the face of Soviet communism in Russia, the rise of Hitler and his supporters in Germany, had seemed, to some on the Right in Britain, a natural development. Some church leaders, not least Bishop Headlam of Gloucester, had even welcomed it. But when, in the second half of the decade, the true nature of Hitler's aims became clear, opinion in political circles divided sharply, and this was reflected in the churches.

One response to the prospect of war was the rise of the Peace Pledge Union, a campaign launched at the Royal Albert Hall in 1935 to oppose rearmament and any thought of fighting. It was led by Dick Sheppard, a charismatic priest who had worked with Temple in the 'Life and Liberty' movement. Sheppard had since been Dean of Canterbury. The PPU gained the support of a wide range of opinion, including C. H. Dodd, Donald MacKinnon and other Christian academics, George MacLeod, Donald Soper and other Christian leaders, George Lansbury of the Labour Party among politicians, Vera Brittain, and non-Christian academics such as Bertrand Russell. As a movement it recalled the horrors of the First World War and was determined they should not be repeated.

It also believed that a gentleman's agreement could be reached with Hitler and Mussolini, an agreement that would make war unnecessary.

The other response was the rejection of pacifism and support for rearmament in the hope that this would deter Hitler. Karl Barth in Switzerland and Reinhold Niebuhr in the United States both rejected pacifism. In Britain this became the majority view among Christians, and this included Temple. In a York diocesan leaflet of November 1935 he once described pacifism as being heretical in tendency. He did not repeat this charge, but during the war he did argue, more persuasively, against a pacifism which saw the taking of German lives as a simple breaking of the law of love. He argued that the question was not simply how Britain could show love to Germans; Britain also needed to show love to Frenchmen, Poles, Czechs and Germans, all at the same time. If it could be said that Britain was fighting to overthrow Nazi tyranny and secure for all Europeans a greater measure of freedom, then resistance to Germany by force was a way of loving Germans themselves as well as others: 'In the world which exists, it is not possible to take it as self-evident that the law of love forbids fighting. Some of us even hold that precisely that law commands fighting.'[39]

In the mid-1930s, however, no one wanted war. Neville Chamberlain's policy of appeasement towards Hitler received widespread support. When, after the Munich agreement of September 1938, he returned to Britain with the infamous words that he had brought back 'peace with honour . . . peace in our time', the nation generally and enthusiastically welcomed it. Most church leaders also welcomed it: Chamberlain was applauded by Cosmo Gordon Lang, the Archbishop of Canterbury, who declared that 'This is the hand of God.' George Bell, Bishop of Chichester, who was in close contact with the German Confessing Christians (who opposed Hitler), and who had protested against the Nazis' arrest of Pastor Niemöller, also agreed with Lang, as did Cardinal Hinsley, the Roman Catholic leader. Temple took the same line. Even the Bishop of Durham, Hensley Henson, who was under no delusions about the true nature of Nazism and its anti-Semitism, was uncomfortably silent.

On 9 November 1938 there was a dramatic change, with *Kristall-nacht*, the burning of 119 synagogues and the arrest of 20,000 Jews in Germany. The true character of Nazi intentions towards the Jews could no longer be ignored. Even so, German church leaders, including the leaders of the Confessing Church, issued no condemnation; nor did Bishop Bell, who took his lead from them. He remained an appeaser even after the declaration of war with Germany. Among the wider public and within the churches, however, the whole atmosphere began to change steadily and determinedly against appeasement. When the Germans invaded the rump of Czechoslovakia, in March 1939, the coming of a European war was finally recognized as being only a matter of time.

The invasion of Poland, of course, finally provoked the outbreak of war. Chamberlain's policy of appeasement was in tatters. The country was now ashamed of the Munich agreement; Lang was dismayed and silent throughout 1939. The turmoil in Europe had compromised all church leaders in one way or another, the pacifists of the PPU as well as the non-pacifists who had turned to appeasement. Even the non-appeasers like Henson who had not risen to the challenge in 1938 were implicated. Adrian Hastings asks: 'What indeed is the peace-seeker to do when faced with "the phenomenon of Hitler"? That question, unanswered then – or answered diversely by equally Christian and conscientious men – remains unanswered still' (Hastings, 1987, p. 343).

Temple was part of all of this: he had accepted appeasement in 1938 (though without the enthusiasm of Lang) and, like other church leaders, had not properly responded to the increasing persecution of the Jews in the 1930s. In these respects he was a creature of his time. But with the outbreak of war between Britain and Germany on 3 September 1939, Temple suddenly and impressively rose to the challenge of the hour. One month after the declaration of war he was invited to give a broadcast to the nation on the BBC. He spoke about the spirit and aims of Britain in the war. He avoided the kind of jingoism that many churchmen had preached at the beginning of the First World War. With his natural and effortless delivery, he spoke with reason and feeling to that grim moment.

Temple began by pointing out the contrast with the atmosphere in August and September 1914, at the outbreak of the First World War, when there had been some high spirits and exhilaration. This time there was less excitement but more resolution. He described how 'for months the public mind has been habituated to the thought that war might become an evident duty'. Now, he said, it

is completely void of excitement. There is a deep determination, accompanied by no sort of exhilaration, but by a
profound sadness. Men are taking up a hateful duty; the very
fact that they hate it throws into greater relief their conviction
that it is a duty. It is a duty first to Poland; but that is rather the
focus than the real essence of our obligation . . . for our
purpose is to check aggression, and to bring to an end the per-
petual insecurity and menace which hang over Europe,
spoiling the life of millions, as a result of the Nazi tyranny in
Germany. (Temple, 1940a, pp. 54–5)

Temple then presented seven shameful events over the last eight
years that showed the criminality of the Nazi regime, the last of
which was the pogrom against the Jews on *Kristallnacht*. He argued
(as Churchill was later to do) that the government should make no
terms with Hitler or his government, because they were simply not
trustworthy. He also argued that whatever terms were made with a
future German government, these should include 'no kind of
advantage for ourselves and no humiliation for the German people'
(Temple, 1940a, p. 57). He finished by calling for a congress of
nations to negotiate eventually a peace agreement.

Temple's words crystallized what many were feeling and
thinking at that moment: he seemed to capture the mood of many
British people, both in their sadness and in their determination to
fight; he presented a clear and powerful account of the causes of the
war; and he was able to lay out reasoned and principled aims for the
conflict. His words, therefore, expressed where people felt they
were, how they had got there, and where they should now aim to go.
It became clear to his listeners that there was a conditional Christian authority behind the declaration of war, and that there was a
clear and commendable aim for the conflict. His address was able
to reassure people and so prepare them for the hard days that lay
ahead.

This broadcast turned Temple into a national leader overnight. It
was heard throughout the British dominions, including Canada
and Australia, giving him an international standing. He seemed to
become the voice of the Christian conscience at a turning point in
British history. This was seen in a small way the following day when
he took the chair at a National Society conference, when Lord
Sankey said: 'Before even the Minutes are read, I want in the name

of all here – and I believe of all Englishmen – to thank our chairman for his broadcast last night' (Iremonger, 1948, p. 541).

The broadcast also made it clear that there was now little doubt that after the retirement of Cosmo Gordon Lang as Archbishop of Canterbury, Temple would replace him. This duly happened in April 1942. Churchill did not admire Temple's views on social reform, nor his lack of bellicosity. He also had no interest in Temple's theology nor in his leadership of the ecumenical movement. Nevertheless, he had no choice but to translate Temple from York to Canterbury. No other bishop in the Church of England had Temple's stature and authority.

Temple and his wife moved from Bishopthorpe in York to Lambeth Palace in London. The enthronement ceremony at Canterbury Cathedral on 23 April 1942 was restrained and in keeping with the conditions of war time. It was one of the lowest points in the war for Britain, but Temple, remarkably but characteristically, spoke of the future with hope. He pointed to the ecumenical movement and described it as 'one great ground of hope for the coming days – this world-wide Christian fellowship, this ecumenical movement, as it is often called' (Temple, 1944, p. 3).

At Lambeth Palace he could only live on the ground floor, as the rest of the house had been badly bombed. He fulfilled his duties while enduring flying bombs by day and air raids by night. He spent more time at Canterbury than his predecessors, but also travelled continually. He would move around the country on crowded buses and trains in the black-out. As Archbishop of Canterbury he became wholly identified with the war effort of the British people.

Confronting social injustice

As the war progressed, the thoughts of many people inevitably turned to the question of what should happen after the fighting was over. What kind of society was going to be rebuilt? How were the resources of the nation going to be distributed? What about health care and education? What about the living conditions in which people would grow up and live? It was well known that the opportunity presented at the end of the First World War, for social reconstruction, had been squandered. What was going to happen this time?

Temple knew that leadership must be provided, and he believed the Church should provide a prophetic kind of leadership on behalf of the poor as well as the rich sections of society. How, though, was he going to rise to this challenge? He began, as the war commenced, before moving from York to Canterbury, by planning the Malvern Conference with P. T. R. Kirk, the director of the Industrial Christian Fellowship. The aim of the Conference would be to consider, from an Anglican standpoint, the fundamental ordering of the new society that was perceived to be emerging from the war effort, and to consider 'how Christian thought could be shaped to play a leading part in the reconstruction after the war is over'. An impressive group of speakers was brought to Malvern for three days in January 1941, including John Middleton Murry, T. S. Eliot, Dorothy Sayers, Sir Richard Acland MP, the philosopher Donald MacKinnon and the social theologian V. A. Demant. There was an array of bishops present and, according to John Kent's researches, about 200 clergy and laity (Kent, 1992, pp. 150, 157).

It was an overloaded programme, and there was little opportunity for discussion. Acland created division among those present with his view that common ownership of the nation's principal industrial resources was a matter of fundamental Christian principle. The issues raised by Demant, MacKinnon and Middleton Murry were not addressed, and by the third day of the Conference the participants were dazed and exhausted. But on the last night, Temple was able to write a series of conclusions, which he then presented to a surprised Conference the following morning, suggesting that they expressed the common mind of the assembly. They were widely welcomed as retrieving some order out of the chaos, except that the resolution on common ownership, the most contentious issue at the Conference, had to be revised. It had reflected Acland's argument about the need for common ownership, and stated that the vesting of the principal industrial resources of the country 'in the hands of private owners is a stumbling block ... contrary to divine justice, making it harder for men to live Christian lives'. The conference members, on an amendment proposed by Bishop Bell, substituted the much vaguer words 'may be' for 'is'. But the final resolution still upheld the important principle that there should be social limits on the freedom of private capitalism.

Despite the poor management of the Conference and the vagueness of the final resolution, the Conference had a wide impact. 'As far as the Church of England was concerned,' writes John Kent,

'Malvern undoubtedly expressed a resurgence of the more radical Anglican attitudes to unemployment and poverty which had dropped into the background after 1926' (Kent, 1992, p. 161). And, as Kent shows, for Temple it was the start of a movement for social reform. This is seen in a letter to Kirk in the month after the Conference where he speaks of 'the movement' and the need to keep a broad range of support behind it, including Anglo-Catholics and Evangelicals, and those in the centre as well as on the left of politics (p. 163).

The increasing strength of the movement is seen the following summer when Kirk informed Temple that the Industrial Christian Fellowship had printed and distributed 200,000 copies of a brief summary of the conclusions of the Conference. Temple went on to write a sixteen-page summary of the Conference, which sold 30,000 copies, and in that same summer planned further meetings in London with a small hand-picked group to discuss practical objectives for reform, the objectives that became 'A Suggested Programme' in *Christianity and Social Order* (see pp. 69–70 of the present work). That book was itself written in the summer and autumn of 1941, and drew on a wide range of theological traditions (giving prominence to the idea of natural law alongside his own Christian social principles), and also of current academic expertise, through consultations with economists such as Keynes, social scientists such as Beveridge, historians such as Tawney, and Stafford Cripps, who later became Chancellor of the Exchequer in the post-war Labour government. Temple was clearly determined to draw up a practicable programme, with radical proposals for eradicating poverty and unemployment, but one which would be supported by a broad range of opinion. He was clearly determined that the opportunity of the moment should not be lost (as it had been lost after the First World War and after the strikes of 1926). He was going to make a deliberate attempt, through consulting, discussing, editing, writing, corresponding and speaking up and down the country, to influence national political life. And all of this on top of his existing duties as an archbishop.

And it began to work. Not only was the Malvern material being bought and read but *Christianity and Social Order* went on to sell 139,000 copies. His social thought was clearly being absorbed by a wider public than the restricted church circles that had previously read his books. And when, in the same year that it was published,

Temple planned some mass meetings to raise the profile of his agenda, he had no trouble in attracting Cripps and Acland, as well as other church leaders, to share his platform. The meetings, organized by Kirk and the ICF, took place at the Albert Hall (September 1942), in Birmingham (November 1942), Leicester (February 1943), Edinburgh (June 1943), and ended with a youth rally back in London (October 1943), all under the title 'The Church Looks Forward'. They created excitement, and the halls were filled with people eager to hear his message.

The first Albert Hall meeting was also to have a much wider significance. Temple took the chair, and spoke. He affirmed, as he had frequently done, the right and the duty of the Church to 'declare its judgment upon social facts and social movements and to lay down principles which should govern the order of society'. Justice was more important than comfort, and the profit motive should never be allowed to predominate in society. There is no harm, he admitted, in the profit motive as such; only when it comes first in the determination of economic and industrial activity is it to be condemned. During the speech he noted how there had been a great amalgamation of banks in the last 50 years, and he pointed to the way that the issuing of credit was becoming monopolized within certain private hands. He continued with words which became notorious:

> Now it is surely a primary political principle that, when something which is universally necessary becomes a monopoly, that monopoly should be taken under public control. In my judgment at least – I don't claim that it is worth much, but I want to offer it you – in my judgment at least it should now be regarded as improper for any person or corporation to issue new credit; as it was in the Middle Ages for any private person or corporation to mint actual money, for the two are equivalent. And so I should like, I confess, to see the banks limited in their lending power to sums equivalent to that which depositors have entrusted to them, and all new credit to be issued by some public authority. (Temple, 1944, p. 112)

The diffident way in which these remarks are made belies the radical nature of their proposals. Temple was advocating a major intervention by the state into the banking system and was proposing that in significant ways it takes command of the financial sector. There was consternation from various quarters of the City of London. It seemed the Archbishop did not know what he was talking about. He was either naive, or an agent for Marxism. What did he think he was proposing? The letters pages of the press became filled, first with protest and then with defence of Temple's words. *The Times* published a selection of letters on several consecutive days, and hardly a newspaper or magazine did not comment. The story was sent around the English-speaking world and publicized in places as far distant from each other as Nebraska and Melbourne. Temple's own mailbag was filled, and so were those of the other speakers that night.

Iremonger glosses over the whole controversy and does not quote the actual criticisms of Temple's opponents. But he does write that in Temple's technical arguments and in his use of technical terms 'there can be little doubt that he went astray. (This becomes even clearer from the many subsequent letters that passed between him and his friends and correspondents among the bankers.)' (Iremonger, 1948, p. 579). According to Iremonger, then, Temple failed to back up his proposals with proper definitions of terms and expert argumentation. It thus became far too easy for his critics to shoot down his proposals.

Or could we assume that his underlying intention was to create a stir? He would not have done this if he had remained narrow and detailed in his proposals. Had he reached a point where there was a need for a dramatic gesture that would graphically place his social concerns squarely on the national political agenda? Was he, in other words, making a prophetic sign to the nation, a sign intended to show the whole way the Christian conscience was confronting the entrenched forces of capitalism with the demand for a more just and equitable world?

Those who supported Temple saw it in this way. Robert Lynd wrote that Temple had 'taken the only step possible to a modern Christian leader in demanding that politics and economics should be christianized' (Iremonger, 1948, p. 581). The cartoon by Low, printed on the front cover of this book, showed that Low believed Temple's views were more than just one proposal for the reform of credit laws. It was instead 'the Christian aim' for post-war reconstruction, in the hands of the Primate of All England, facing down the bulldogs of high finance. And the *Spectator* wrote that the 'effect of the controversy, indeed, is to impress on many people who had overlooked it that the new Primate is a man of great knowledge and brilliant intellect, as well as of abundant moral courage.' It also thought that support for Temple's speech far outweighed the criticism it evoked (Iremonger, 1948, p. 581).

Temple himself saw his banking proposals, naively perhaps, as nothing more than his own personal views given to illustrate the principles on which a Christian social order could be founded. But, as many pointed out, it was impossible for the Archbishop of Canterbury just to give his own personal views. He was too big and too important for that. Nevertheless, through the controversy, he stood his ground and said that he had issued his challenge to stir consciences and provoke attention (Iremonger, 1948, p. 582). This confirms a prophetic intention behind his words and actions.

Did the Albert Hall speech, and the campaign that followed it, complete and crown the prophetic movement that had begun at Malvern, or did it undermine its credibility? Did Temple become a prophet to the nation, or was he just an attention-seeking bishop who did not know what he was talking about? The answer to this question will depend on one's own perceptions and values. More recent commentators have tended to side with Temple's critics at this point. Norman, for example, calls Temple's views on banking 'absurd' (1976, p. 323). Hastings calls them 'a bee in his bonnet' (1987, p. 398).[40] His supporters at the time, as we have seen, thought he was doing what was right. Perhaps, paradoxically, such difference of opinion confirms his prophetic status, for prophecy tends to divide those who hear it.

The final verdict can rest with the younger generation who were present at the time and who did not have vested interests on one side or the other. One voice comes from the religious and political left wing, and the other voice from the right. On the left is David Jenkins, who later became the Bishop of Durham and himself no stranger to controversy. At the centenary of Temple's birth, in 1981, he wrote the following autobiographical words in the journal *Theology*:

As a teenager I attended the Albert Hall meeting which Temple addressed, along with others including Sir Stafford Cripps, and what I drew from this, as well as what I read of his utterances and writings, was a clear understanding that we should be deeply Christian and deeply concerned with current affairs. Christianity was neither a purely private religion nor a merely spiritual religion. This was so because of the nature and purposes of the God to whom Christianity was a response. Temple was, surely, a powerfully devout man, and the demands which he put before one were clearly religious, devotional, and godly. But godliness required concern for the affairs of society because men and women were so socially shaped, and often socially distorted, and because the transcendent God was committed to worldly particularities for the furthering of his purposes and the sharing of his love. (*Theology*, September 1981, pp. 321–2)

There is not much here about Temple's views on banking but, instead, the subject of the reminiscences is the whole orientation of the Christian towards the world in which he or she lives. Temple's words at the Albert Hall did not make Jenkins question Temple's credibility but, rather, inspired him to enter into the struggles of making society conform more closely to the love of God. For Jenkins, at least, Temple had become a prophet of God's transforming will for this world.

On the right wing Edward Heath expressed similar sentiments:

The impact of William Temple on my generation was immense . . . The reason was not far to seek. William Temple was foremost among the leaders of the nation, temporal or spiritual, in posing challenging, radical questions about the nature of our society. Most important of all, he propounded with lucidity and vigour his understanding of the Christian ethic in its application to the contemporary problems which engrossed us all. (Temple, 1976, Foreword)

The movement which had begun at Malvern, then, and which led, through *Christianity and Social Order*, to 'The Church Looks Forward', clearly touched and inspired a great many people, from a variety of standpoints, to pick up the torch offered by Temple. If further proof of his historic significance was needed, the constructive work of the post-war government in Britain can be cited. Within the space of five years many of the social and economic objectives advocated by Temple had been achieved. These included the creation of a National Health Service, the nationalization of principal industrial resources such as the coal industry, and major improvements in social security. Taken as a whole, this amounted to the creation of the welfare state. There were, of course, other powerful forces behind these developments, but William Temple and those who supported him showed that the Christian Church was both an impressive herald and an instrument of their coming. In a significant way he and they were prophets of the post-war society in Britain in which, in these respects, there was greater social justice for ordinary people.

Intervening in politics again

The confronting of social injustice was the most significant aspect of Temple's work as Archbishop of Canterbury, but not the only one. He held a vast range of other interests and causes, some of which he had adopted when still at York. He wrote many letters to the press on different subjects, and a vast range of other correspondence with government ministers, ambassadors and civil servants. He probably over-extended his patronage and made it less effective than it could have been, but some of the support he gave was politically and morally significant.

He would be informed, for example, of the plight of an individual or group in mainland Europe. At one point it was the threat of famine to the people of Belgium. On another occasion it was the fate of an individual German pastor. At another point the increasingly horrific plight of the Jews was brought to his attention. In response to the first group he gave his support to the efforts of Bishop Bell to secure famine relief, trying to get around the block which the Foreign Office put in their path when it said that any relief must not 'help the enemy'. With regard to the German pastor, who had been arrested by the Nazis, he began correspondence in November 1939 and was still writing letters in 1942. On the plight of the Jews, his response was emphatic: when, towards the end of 1942, it was confirmed that there was a deliberate Nazi plan to exterminate the Jews of Europe, and that during that year most of Poland's three million Jews had already been wiped out, Temple wrote at once to *The Times* expressing 'burning indignation at this atrocity, to which the records of barbarous ages scarcely supply a parallel' (5 December).

It was then up to the Allies to attempt to rescue those Jews who were yet to be sent to the camps. Those in Bulgaria, Hungary and Rumania would have been the easiest to save. Churchill would have liked to do something, but his expressed wishes were disregarded. It seems that the Allies thought that large numbers of Jewish refugees could only become a nuisance in whichever country they were given asylum (Hastings, 1987, pp. 376–7).

Temple had at first tried to put pressure on the government with private correspondence, to the foreign secretary, the colonial secretary and the Prime Minister: What was the government going to do about this outrage? In reply, ministers tried to divert Temple with their own questions: 'Had the Archbishop considered the possibility of an anti-Semitic outbreak in England which might follow on from some special favour being shown to Jews?' Or, 'Was there not the danger of giving Hitler an excuse for further barbarities if he could point to British acts of charity and tell his people that the Jews were now seen to be the friends of Britain and therefore the enemies of the Fatherland?' (Iremonger, 1948, p. 565).

At last, on 23 March 1943, Temple publicly called for action. In a long and significant speech in the House of Lords, one of his most important in that chamber, he moved a motion calling for 'immediate measures, on the largest and most generous scale compatible with the requirements of military operation and security, for providing help and temporary asylum to persons in danger of massacre who are able to leave enemy and enemy-occupied countries'. Temple quoted figures of the massacre and torture of the Jews 'before which the imagination recoils', and made several suggestions for government action, including the appointment of a senior official to oversee the measures. He concluded,

> We know that what we can do is small compared with the magnitude of the problem, but we cannot rest so long as there is any sense among us that we are not doing all that might be done . . . We at this moment have upon us a tremendous responsibility. We stand at the bar of history, of humanity, and of God. (Iremonger, 1948, pp. 566–7)

The government's reply, as always, was that the best way of helping the Jews was winning the war, and all the attention of the government should be on this rather than special relief efforts for those

Jews imprisoned by Hitler. Temple's response to this hopeless line of reasoning was not to slacken his efforts but to continue with writing letters and pressing for action. Whether or not his vociferous intervention would be effective at any given moment, 'it ought to be said for the sake of the principles of justice itself, and I shall continue the advocacy which I have endeavoured to offer hitherto' (Iremonger, 1948, p. 567).

The political importance of Temple's stand, in the midst of the Holocaust, should not be over-emphasized. He was not effective in getting the British government to do anything very significant about the concentration camps: even the railway lines to the camps were never bombed. But his was still a morally important attempt to provoke action; it was recognized as such by the World Jewish Congress on Temple's death. An official statement from that body said that he would be 'particularly mourned by the Jewish people whose champion he was . . . Profoundly conscious of the physical suffering of the Jews, and acutely sensitive to its spiritual significance, he was at all times ready to make every contribution to the alleviation of the great tragedy that had befallen a great people' (Iremonger, 1948, p. 567).

*   *   *

Much more controversial were Temple's views on the Allied strategy of obliteration bombing. This strategy became known to the British public in the middle of 1943. It was clear that many thousands of German civilians would be killed as Allied bombs flattened the centres of different cities. Bishop Bell asked Temple for support in his campaign to stop it. Bell's argument was that 'to bomb cities as cities, deliberately to attack civilians, quite irrespective of whether or not they are actively contributing to the war effort, is a wrong deed, whether done by the Nazis or by ourselves' (Hastings, 1987, p. 378). This stand was deeply unpopular at the time and Bell became a *persona non grata* in the corridors of power for the rest of the war. Some believe that it may have cost him preferment to Canterbury after Temple's death. But, subsequently, as the awfulness and ineffectiveness of the obliteration bombing has become generally known, Bell's costly stand has become correspondingly admired and respected.

Temple's position, on the other hand, has come to seem less

impressive. He refused to support Bell on this issue: 'I am not at all disposed to be the mouthpiece of the concern which I know exists, because I do not share it' (Hastings, 1987, p. 377). To another correspondent he explained that

> I wrote . . . to the Secretary of State for Air to ask if he could assure me that the principles governing [the Allied] choice of objectives remained unaltered, and he replied that they were unaltered. All that has changed is the scale; and that seems to me irrelevant, except as a factor to balance against the probable gain. If it appeared that this method of warfare – always directed to the checking of the enemy's war effort – led to a break up of the enemy's war machine without the years of slaughter probably involved in an invasion of Germany on land, it would seem to me certainly justified – supposing we are justified in fighting at all. (Temple, 1963, p. 103)

Temple, then, saw no moral differentiation between the bombing of German cities and the kind of bombing that had preceded it. He believed the government when it said that military objectives were still determining the strategy. The only judgement to be made was a military one, as to whether this type of bombing would actually bring the war to a swifter conclusion. On this type of judgement Temple did not have or claim any expertise and so was unwilling to oppose the strategy. Subsequent findings have questioned the military effectiveness of the strategy, but Temple could not have known these, and so at one level Temple's reasoning cannot be questioned.

In another letter, on 30 August, he admitted that talking about this issue in these ways 'always seems horribly cold-blooded in view of the horrible facts with which one is dealing'. But he maintained his position, arguing that the strategy was justified because it was directed to military objectives even though there were inevitable tragic consequences in the deaths of civilians. On the other hand, a strategy of dropping bombs 'merely with the object of killing the general population would not be legitimate' (Temple, 1963, pp. 106–7).

In his own terms it seems that Temple cannot be criticized. He was not aware of any good reason to question the government's word when it said the bombing was not intended primarily to kill the civilian population, and so he saw no reason to oppose the strategy on moral grounds. But, compared to Bell, Temple can be criticized for a lack of imagination on this issue. Bell had been wrong about Hitler's true intentions,[41] and wrong about the effectiveness of appeasement, but on this issue he was impressively right: he imaginatively grasped what obliteration bombing really meant on the ground, as opposed to what it meant in the heads of Allied military strategists. He saw that it amounted to killing the general civilian population for its own sake, and with undeniable courage and at cost to himself, he said as much. The government failed to take heed and, on this occasion, so did William Temple.

★   ★   ★

There was one other way in which Temple significantly intervened in political affairs. This time it was on the domestic issue of education, one that had been close to his heart since WEA days. During the middle years of the war, R. A. Butler, who was president of the Board of Education, set about drawing up proposals for a new national framework for schools, to come into effect at the end of the war. Up to this point schooling had been divided between church schools, whether Church of England or Nonconformist or Roman Catholic, and schools funded by the state. In the inter-war years the funding of state schools had significantly overtaken that of the church schools, and many church schools had fallen into a poor state of health, not only in the quality of the teaching but in the state of the buildings. The Church of England alone had 400 school buildings on the Board's blacklist. Up to now, however, the churches had sought to keep a distance from the state in order to preserve the religious character of the education they were providing, and they had kept their distance from each other in order to preserve their denominational identity. It was now clear that they seriously lacked the resources to bring their own schools up to national standards. What was to be done?

Butler published his proposals on educational reconstruction in July 1943; he published a Bill to go to Parliament in the following December. He proposed, significantly, raising the school leaving age to 16, and maintaining the dual system, but with the state and the churches co-ordinating the services they provided. This meant that both the churches and the state would provide education for whoever lived near their schools, and the church schools would be brought into a national framework. The churches would also have to make sure their schools achieved certain minimum standards. This would be expensive, but Butler also proposed that the state would fund 50 per cent of the cost of modernizing and maintaining the church schools. Furthermore, he proposed that it now be compulsory for state schools to provide for an act of worship in the school each day, and that religious instruction be included within the state curriculum (though parents could withdraw their children from this if they wanted). The Bill therefore represented a certain amount of give and take for both the churches and the state. It would require some new funding from the churches for their schools, but it would also bring significant extra funding from the state.

When the Bill was published there was concern from the Nonconformists that in some areas their children would have to attend a Church of England school. Also, from some non-church teachers in the state system there was consternation that they would have to lead prayers. The last Bill to propose education reform, the Birrell Bill of 1906, had been wrecked by quarrelling between the churches. What would happen this time?

Two views quickly developed. Many in the educational world, including a number of Temple's colleagues in the WEA, hated the idea of a dual system of education, with the continued existence of church schools: there should be one modern system for all children. On the other hand, many in the churches were unhappy with the idea of relinquishing to the state some of the control of their own schools. Temple took neither view but instead wholeheartedly supported the idea of a co-ordinated dual system. He saw that the churches were simply not able to maintain their schools on their own and they must start to work with the state as partners. But he also believed in the dual system in its own right. To a WEA conference in February 1944 he described his ideal. He argued that there be schools of a variety of types with a considerable measure of individual autonomy. So he believed that Butler was offering a positive and generous way forward for church schools and, equally importantly, he believed that the general raising of the school leaving age to 16 was a significant step forward for English society as a whole. When he spoke to his diocesan conference in Canterbury in October, supporting Butler's proposals, this was the point he emphasized above all others: 'it is the most essential element of the Bill' (Iremonger, 1948, pp. 573, 575).

Temple spoke for the Bill in the Church Assembly, which accepted it. He chaired meetings with Nonconformist educationalists so that agreement on some of the details of the Bill could be reached. He also spoke to church and non-church audiences up and down the country advocating its proposals. R. H. Tawney movingly describes one such address:

> The last public gathering at which I heard Temple speak was a conference of representatives of Labour and educational organisations, with Sir Walter Citrine in the chair, to demand the passage of the Bill at any early date. He was greatly over-burdened at the time and, as usual, arrived late. He spoke simply, avoiding technical details, and making no attempt to give the impression of special knowledge. The effect of his speech on the audience was due to his transparent sincerity and to the fervour of moral conviction with which he spoke: it was, I think, profound. (Iremonger, 1948, p. 575)

Temple's final advocacy for the Bill was in the House of Lords. One of those who was there reported that his speeches for the Bill 'were notably successful and he spoke with great authority' (Iremonger, 1948, p. 577). When the Bill returned to the House of Commons, in a two-day debate, 20 out of the 31 speeches were concerned with the religious issue, which showed how important it was. But there was none of the bitterness between denominational traditions that had wrecked the Birrell Bill. In the end, the main parts of the Bill were all passed, including the requirement to have a daily act of corporate worship in state schools.

Temple's final act of political intervention, then, was notably successful and important. It was very different from his first foray into politics as a bishop in 1926. The Education Act of 1944 belonged to Butler, but Temple's support at his right hand was crucially important in ensuring that its proposals became law, and it was fitting, perhaps, that Temple's career should conclude on the issue with which it had begun – education.

Temple did not himself see his career finishing at this point. The next step, he believed, was proper provision of adult education, and he became involved with setting up a central organization to help local authorities have the resources and skills they needed to provide the kind of rich and diverse educational opportunities the 1944 Act was requiring. Sadly, his death in October 1944 prevented him from taking this work forward.

CHAPTER 8

In the End

Last days

During the years of war Temple steadily increased his level of public engagements. At York he had had time to prepare the Gifford Lectures and the *Readings in St John*. When he moved to Canterbury there was no time for writing or academic lecturing. The only volume to be published was a collection of sermons and addresses, a book which took its title from 'The Church Looks Forward' campaign. He felt that with so many men and women in the armed services giving their lives to the service of their country, he could hardly do less himself. And so he would speak as often and in as many places as the hours of the day would allow him. Between speaking he would write his letters, in his own hand, to everyone who wrote to him, and to many others as well.

On one occasion in Coventry, between 4 p.m. and 10 p.m., Temple spoke at three meetings and attended a reception. There was an interval of 50 minutes in the six hours and this, his host reports, he filled by writing letters, fourteen in all. Randall Davidson had had the measure of Temple many years earlier when he said, 'The trouble with dear William is, he is so kind that he cannot say No.' This became even more true during the years at Canterbury.

He loved the work, of course. Julian Huxley wrote how Temple was due to attend a meeting in central London on the day a terrifying daylight air raid took place. The meeting had to take place in a basement shelter that was not particularly safe:

After a quarter of an hour, during which the elements of a snack lunch were provided, Temple appeared, his arrival heralded down the basement stairs by characteristic gusts of laughter. I don't think that we got much further that day in the definition of war aims, but I do know that Temple's presence acted as a vivifying tonic on every human being present in that by no means agreeable situation, from the youngest typist up to the research director. (Iremonger, 1948, p. 619)

All this work inevitably took its toll. It had begun to do so before he moved to Canterbury. To his brother, in 1941, he confided: 'We have kept our Silver Wedding here to-day in great restfulness; we are both tired, so having kept the day clear we slept nearly all the afternoon in the garden' (Iremonger, 1948, p. 506). In the last couple of years his gout began to return more regularly and each time more painfully; and it was not helped by the disturbed nights at Lambeth, with flying bombs frequently falling nearby. Temple had to sleep on a sofa in the ground-floor passage of the palace, where there was a domed roof which had so far stood up to the shock of bomb explosions near by. One bomb explosion was so close it blew off the back door of the palace as well as blowing in countless windows. Temple commented to his brother that 'Of course it all causes much inconvenience, but for us nothing worse than that, so far, and this hideous house stands like the Rock of Gibraltar!' Iremonger reports, though, that when the bomb fell, Temple had just finished shaving and was getting ready for his bath. He scrambled out into the passage, and a second later a good part of the ceiling collapsed (1948, p. 620).

But he did take holidays, and he and his wife most frequently visited the Isle of Wight, the Lake District, the valley of the Kennet, and the Quantocks. In the Lakes he would always wear an old Norfolk jacket whose original colour might have been anything from grey to green. Sandwiches would stick out of one pocket, maps from another, and on his head an old hat with holes in it. He would forge slowly up the fell tracks, but liked to leap down them on the way back (at least when he was younger). After the walks his companions remembered his appetite for tremendous farmhouse teas of bread and butter, cream, bilberry jam and apple pastry. One of his fellow-walkers wrote what has become a famous story of a walk at Buttermere:

William knew the Lakes intimately and was a stalwart and steady walker. Having more to carry he progressed more slowly than the rest of us. One hot morning Tawney, Bell [not the bishop], and I, having reached the summit of Great Gable, watched William climbing steadily upwards and 'larding the lean earth' as he came. When he reached the rock on which we were sitting, he sat heavily down, wiped his brow and exclaimed: 'Thank God, I do *not* believe in the resurrection of the *flesh!*' (Iremonger, 1948, p. 508)

That was before the move to Canterbury. In these years he and his wife would get away on their own, especially to a holiday cottage at Weacombe in Somerset, for rest and the opportunity to be with each other. They talked of his retirement and he of his plans to write a book on the Holy Spirit. But the gout returned when he was back at work: it always seemed to do so when he was under great pressure.

At the beginning of September 1944 it returned again, this time more severely than ever before. He was unable to use his legs and had to be carried into Canterbury Cathedral when the clergy of the diocese assembled for a synod. This meeting had been planned for months and he was determined to give his address. In this, his last public engagement, he spoke of the need for the clergy to find inward strengthening through regular prayer, meditation, penitence and retreats, for '"Apart from Me, ye can do nothing."' He then urged the parochial clergy to undertake evangelism; such evangelism should be directed especially towards those men and women who would be returning from war service and whose habits of a lifetime had been broken by the war. He asked deaneries to establish evangelism committees, and parishes to call groups of men and women to visit and encourage the returnees to respond. He told the clergy that if ever they thought that he could help them in any difficulties of their own they were to let him know, and 'if you would at all like to come and talk them over, ask for an appointment without any hesitation. It may have to be fixed for some weeks ahead, for my engagement book gets very full; but it can always be arranged. After all, it is what I am here for!' (Temple, 1963, p. 182).

And he issued a pastoral letter, to be read at the main service in all the parishes, calling on all parishioners to share in this great evangelistic calling. In the letter, in characteristic vein, he wrote how God:

was putting before us a great opportunity. Let us all dedicate ourselves anew and pray for the guidance and strength of His Holy Spirit that we may use this time, when a new fashion of life must needs be formed, in the way that will most set forward His glory and the true welfare of all His people. (Temple, 1963, p. 185)

Three days later he wrote to his brother that the attack of gout had returned 'in prodigious violence, and I have now got acute gout in both knees, which, as you can imagine, is quite immobilising . . . at present I am able to make no plans' (Temple, 1963, p. 187). Nevertheless, over the next two days he saw some ordination candidates while sitting up in bed, and then called them all to sit round him while he delivered his address to them. This was his last ministerial act.

Two young girls, Zoë and Nancy Brennan, knowing that Temple was ill, took some grapes to his house. He was emphatic that the grapes should not be put on a plate but left in the children's basket, just as they had brought them, and he sent them this reply:

Dear Zoë and Nancy

I am sorry to be so late in writing to thank you for so kindly sending me those grapes. It has not been easy to write till now, and even to-day I cannot do much. But the horrid thing does seem to be going away and though I still have a lot of discomfort, the really bad pain seems to be over.

Thank you so much.

Yours sincerely,

William Cantuar

(Temple, 1963, p. 190)

He was then taken for rest and treatment to Westgate, where he remained. His sixty-third birthday fell on 15 October. A few days later he wrote to Lang (the retired archbishop), that the gout was being kept alive by a sub-acute streptococcal infection, and that this must be tackled first. However, there was to be no chance to do that. On 26 October, in the morning, he was struck by a pulmonary embolism caused by a blood clot. He said that he felt very faint and his wife hurried to get help. A doctor was at hand and did what he could. '"Are you in great pain?" he asked, to which Temple replied: "No, but I can't breathe"' (Iremonger, 1948, p. 625). A few minutes later he was dead.

★   ★   ★

News of his death was met with shock and disbelief in Britain and around the world. His funeral took place in Canterbury Cathedral a few days later and then, as he had wished, he was cremated. His ashes were laid beside the grave of his father in the cloisters at Canterbury.

A calling to prophecy

Temple has always been a difficult person to assess. The first commentators, writing after the shock of his premature death, tended to present an uncritical portrait. The obituaries and books that come from the late 1940s and 1950s present his achievements without dwelling on his weaknesses. Iremonger's biography is a good example of this genre: it presents Temple's life in such glowing terms that the end result is but a two-dimensional portrait. Yet the book is still a goldmine of information and insight. From the 1960s to the mid-1980s there was an inevitable reaction, with criticism predominating.[42] Owen C. Thomas investigated Temple's philosophy of religion and found it problematic.[43] John Carmichael and Harold Goodwin wrote a narrowly focused book on the political and sociological ideas of four of his books and, from their right-wing perspective, were scathing in their assessment.[44] A. R. Vidler (in 1976) wrote an article dwelling on Temple's limitations as a theologian and as a person, questioning the breadth of his spiritual insight, and writing, as we have seen, that 'Temple was a theologian for Christmas rather than for Passiontide'.[45] E. R. Norman criticized Temple for being too idealistic in politics and for failing to translate his social thought into 'realities'.[46] John Rogerson, as we have seen, found his philosophical theology built on a questionable theodicy (see pp. 29–30). Alan Suggate, in his ethics-focused book of 1987, questioned Temple's social thought and especially his social principles, generally preferring Reinhold Niebuhr's approach.[47]

It was Adrian Hastings, in his acclaimed *History of English Christianity 1920–1985* (1986), in a sympathetic lecture of 1992, 'William Temple', and now in his entry on William Temple in the forthcoming *New Dictionary of National Biography*, who has allowed a more balanced and impressive picture of the man to begin to re-emerge. This picture places Temple within the context of his times so that his real achievements can be seen alongside his limitations. Hastings has remained critical of Temple in certain important ways, especially for his reluctance to take sides when there were unbridgeable divisions, and for his avoidance of any sustained disagreement with government policy, especially in the 1930s and over obliteration bombing during the war. Yet in the end, Hastings says it would be hard to think of any other twentieth-century ecclesiastical figure whose impact on history has been comparable, certainly in England, possibly in the world. Hastings places Temple in the company of Winston Churchill, Bertrand Russell and George Bernard Shaw as one of the leading figures in the British society of his generation, 'among whom he might well be judged the most balanced in mind, the most consistent throughout a long career, and, certainly, the most personally loved'.[48] Yet how is such a figure to be characterized within national and ecclesiastical life? Should it be as an ecclesiastical statesman like Randall Davidson, or as an influential social theologian like Reinhold Niebuhr, or as a great reformer like William Wilberforce or Lord Shaftesbury? Such a judgement needs to be based on an extended reappraisal of Temple's life, which Hastings has not written. So a key question remains unanswered for the assessment of Temple in our own day.

The most recent book on Temple, John Kent's *William Temple: Church, State and Society in Britain 1880–1950*, starts by agreeing with Hastings that Temple was one of the most remarkable Christian leaders of the twentieth century. Kent, however, does not write a rounded biography but concentrates on Temple's political impact in Church and state, and this inevitably leads to a one-sided presentation. He is very critical of the consensus-building type of approach to national and church politics favoured by Temple. At the end of the book Temple is criticized for embodying an approach that failed, in the 1980s, to stem the resurgence of the right wing in British politics. The fact that Temple's approach resulted in many of the 'left-wing' achievements of 1945–1951 government seems, oddly, less significant to Kent.[49]

Temple, then, is an important but difficult figure to sum up. At the end of his 1992 lecture Hastings compared Temple with Charles Gore and Michael Ramsey, two other twentieth-century Anglican figures who combined theological influence with practical leadership. 'Temple remains the man 'in the middle', his time cut off in war, still the most enigmatic of the three, the most difficult to make up one's mind about' (Hastings, 1995, p. 68).

Much of the story told by this book confirms this statement. The range of his interests was vast, the energy with which he pursued them staggering, and the results of his work a remarkable litany of achievement. And yet, when each strand is examined in its own right, he seems to become like the French people, 'Great in all the arts, supreme in none.' His philosophical theology was impressive in its scope and accomplished in its expression, and yet, as we have seen, did not quite succeed in achieving the goal it set itself. His leadership and reform of the Church, in the 'Life and Liberty' movement, then as a diocesan bishop, then Archbishop, was important in updating some of the structures (the dividing of the diocese of Manchester being the clearest example), but it did not institute and carry through a general reform of the Church of England. His successor, Archbishop Fisher, would do more of this than he. Temple's work for social reform, whether through COPEC or the Malvern Conference, or even 'The Church Looks Forward' campaign, did not bring *direct* results in the way that Wilberforce, say, had done, though it did have a significant general influence. His interventions in the politics of his time were few and far between (compared with Davidson's), and for most of his career (up to the outbreak of the Second World War) relatively meagre in their results. His role in the emergent ecumenical movement was crucial, along with that of J. H. Oldham and William Paton, but his contribution was essentially one of bringing people together and building bridges between them, rather than creating the ecumenical ideal in the first place. He did not plant the ecumenical movement, although he certainly watered it. And his work as a Christian social theologian, while important as an example of practical theology in making connections between philosophy and theology on the one hand, and social and economic policies on the other, did not itself create an influential school of thought in the way that Niebuhr or Jacques Maritain had done. Temple was great in so many ways, possibly more ways than any other contemporary church person in Britain or around the world, but supreme in none of them.

Nevertheless, this kind of statement does not capture the full significance of the man. There was something about the way he combined all these things which suggests that there was more to him than the sum of these different parts. Hastings puts it this way: 'There have been more convincing philosophical theologians, more effective social reformers, greater preachers, more-single-minded ecumenists, but no one who combined all these skills to so high a degree and who so steadily matched his leadership with the hour.'[50] It was something to do with the way Temple used his gifts and position to move things forward that was so significant. Through his missions to universities, campaigning work around the country, pastoral work as a bishop, writing, speaking, letter-writing and chairmanship, and his national leadership, he not only presented an ideal, but moved people towards its realization. In particular, he seemed to present God's new world in Christ, in both words and in the visible integrity and holiness of his life, and he inspired large numbers of people to conform their lives, and the life of their society, to its nature. He seemed to bring God's reign near to people, and to bring them nearer to God's reign, within the Church of England, within British society, and within European and worldwide church life.

His real significance, in other words, lay in the prophetic character of his life: he became a herald and instrument of God's kingdom. He did this obviously at certain moments of his life, such as in the 1931 Oxford Mission, and in the campaign against social injustice in the 1940s, but he did it generally in the whole way he came to embody God's reign in his work and being.

Such an assessment should not be surprising. Through the course of this book we have seen a prophetic ministry come to expression, from the call he received as an undergraduate, through various struggles to express it, to a growth in authority and stature in the Church and nation. We saw that for some periods of his life the calling lay dormant, with other interests coming to the fore, while at other moments, as in 1926, he tried with others to be prophetic but failed with some embarrassment. But from 1931 onwards we saw a kind of fulfilment, in his student missions, his work for the ecumenical movement, his support for the reform of education, but most notably in the campaign that began at Malvern and grew through *Christianity and Social Order* to the climax of 'The Church Looks Forward'. Through this campaign he set out to be prophetic and, by many, was heard to be prophetic, with significant results after his death. It was the defining moment of his life: everything he had done and everything he had become combined to issue a powerful and graphic call to the British public. With great authority he set before people an ideal for society as a whole, and moved them towards its realization, so much so that he has been credited with being one of the founders of the social reforms of post-war British society.

William Temple was a prophet, albeit a rather reasonable, jovial and consensus-seeking one. This is the secret of his identity and ultimate achievements. It is the term that Bishop George Bell of Chichester, Temple's friend and fellow-worker (with whom he occasionally disagreed), chose to sum him up.[51] And, as Iremonger wrote, such an identity explains the 'ceaseless and deliberate progress from one platform and pulpit to another, this complete dedication to an ideal, this certitude in believing and assurance in uttering the word he felt bound to proclaim' (1948, p. 516). Temple occupied a multitude of different roles through his life, but the connecting thread was the way he continually spoke about and lived out the hope of a new world (and not just of a new Church). He believed this to be God's kingdom revealed in Christ. To the injustices and decay of the old world he presented the liberty and assurance of the new, and he encouraged and inspired his fellow human beings, both within and beyond the churches, to reach out for such a world themselves.

It is because he was a prophet that Temple has an enduring significance. His life and work is itself a calling to prophecy: by seeming to embody the marvellous reality of God's new world he intrinsically invites us to do as he did. By showing the holiness and warmth of what God has promised to the world, his life of itself calls us also to become heralds and instruments of that promise. Bishop Bell described Temple as having 'all the vividness and swiftness of a flame . . . he communicated warmth and light to all who saw or heard him.'[52] We can still feel that warmth and light. It calls us too, in the changed circumstances of today, to become prophets of God's kingdom to the whole world.

Notes

1 The affectionate way in which Frederick Temple regarded his sons is also shown in Peter Hinchliff, *Frederick Temple* (1998) pp. 162–5.

2 Quoted in Duncan Forbes, *The Liberal Anglican Idea of History* (1952) pp. 66–8.

3 *Lay Sermons and Addresses delivered in the Hall of Balliol College,* Glasgow (1908) pp. 70–1. For an overview of Green and Caird's religious thought see Peter Hinchliff, 'Cut Loose from History: British Idealism and the Science of Religion', in *God and History* (1992).

4 In 'Robert Browning', an essay read at Balliol, reprinted in *Religious Experience* (1958) p. 33.

5 The letters are reprinted in Iremonger (1948) pp. 115–21.

6 Letter to Ford, reprinted in Iremonger (1948) p. 133.

7 John Kent sees Temple's lack of success as a headmaster as illustrating the weakness of the argument he was using in the Oxford Mission to prove the reality of divine guidance (Kent, *William Temple* (1992) pp. 183–4). But, as we have argued, why could not God have guided him to Repton to show that following the path of his father was not to be the way for him?

8 'Freedom of Conscience', in *The Challenge*, No. 103 (14 April 1916). See also No. 183 (26 October 1917), No. 188 (30 November 1917). The last article upholds the right of conscientious objectors to vote.

9 For a discussion of *Foundations* as a whole see Peter Hinchliff, *God and History* (1992) pp. 232–44. Hinchliff emphasizes the variety of theological opinion found in its different essays.

10 *A History of English Christianity 1920–1985* (1987) p. 232.

11 In 'William Temple as Philosopher and Theologian' (1981) pp. 330–3.

12 See Iremonger (1948) pp. 256–7, though Adrian Hastings thinks that Davidson would have supported what became known as the Enabling Act even if 'Life and Liberty' had not existed. See his article on William Temple in the forthcoming *New Dictionary of National Biography.*

13 See Williams (1993) *Viewed from the Water Tank,* p. 27.

14 For these and more details see Williams (1993) pp. 51–4.

15 See Iremonger (1948) pp. 305–7.

16 For a more extended discussion of the connections between Temple's theology

and philosophy see J. W. Rogerson, 'Willam Temple as Philosopher and Theologian' (1981).

17   'The Limitations of William Temple' (1976) p. 38.

18   A. R. Peacocke has described William Temple's percipience in detecting those broad features in the new knowledge of his day – mostly from the sciences – that theology needed properly to respond to. See 'The New Biology and *Nature, Man and God'* (1983) p. 29.

19   Iremonger (1948) pp. 333, 509. Temple continued to feel more sympathy with the Labour Party's general programme than with that of any other political group, though he was not always ready to give Labour leaders the active help they sought from him (pp. 509–10).

20   From 'Christian Social Principles', *The Pilgrim* (1921) reprinted in *Essays in Christian Politics* (1927) pp. 9–10.

21   p. 85. For a more detailed discussion of the philosophical foundations of Temple's social thought see my dissertation, *The Decline of Historicism in William Temple's Social Thought* (1990) especially Chapter 2, 'History'. For a summary see my 'History and Society in William Temple's Thought' (1992).

22   For an assessment of *Christianity and Social Order* and especially of the political theory inherent in its pages see my '*Christianity and Social Order* after Fifty Years' (1992).

23   *Christianity and the State* (1928) pp. 123–4. See Chapter 3, Section III, 'The State', in my dissertation, for an analysis of Temple's evolving views of the state. In 1905, in *The Education of Citizens,* he advanced a crude state-collectivism, but in the Henry Scott Holland lectures he had come to advocate a more limited understanding of the authority and role of the state in society.

24   'William Temple – An Appreciation' (1945) p. 45.

25   For a longer discussion of Temple's use of the term 'equality' see Chapter 4, Section III 'Equality', in my D.Phil dissertation.

26   Temple made the following comment on Tawney's book *Equality*: 'I agree about Tawney. To be quite truthful I was bitterly disappointed with *Equality*. The whole of the main contention could have been put on to ten pages. And the sustained, rather contemptuous, irony infects the whole style. It is one of the worst written books that I ever saw from the pen of a capable writer.' William Temple Papers, Vol. 30, p. 230.

27   See, for example, his 'Middle Axioms in Christian Social Ethics' in *Explorations in Theology 9* (1981).

28   See p. 35. Maurice Bruce writes that it was probably the Oxford economist Alfred Zimmern who coined the term as a deliberate contrast to 'the Power State' of the Fascist dictators. See *The Coming of the Welfare State* (1961) p. 31.

29   'The Real Meaning of the War', from a series of unpublished articles (1941), in the William Temple Papers, Vol. 67, p. 125.

30   Reprinted in John Kent, *William Temple* (1992) p. 125.

31   See John Kent, *William Temple* (1992) pp. 138, 139, 142.

32   Reprinted in *Essays in Christian Politics,* p. 192.

33   These were aspects of the Anglican Church that Temple was not prepared to surrender in ecumenical discussions. He welcomed the exchange of pulpits between ministers of the different churches, but he could not accept the interchangeability of eucharistic ministry. On his belief that, technically, the eucharistic ministry of the non-Catholic churches was irregular, and that episcopacy was necessary to the preservation of the true Order of the Church, he

was vigorously challenged by Reinhold Niebuhr. See Niebuhr's fascinating account of their discussions in Iremonger (1948) pp. 493–4.

34 From 'William Temple', in the forthcoming *New Dictionary of National Biography*. All the information in this paragraph is from Hastings.

35 'The Genesis of the World Council of Churches' (1968) p. 713.

36 *William Temple* (1992) pp. 99–109. Kent emphasizes the failure of the provisional committee of the WCC to get agreement from the European churches about war aims and peace aims in the conflict. But the very existence of such a committee within the broader context of twentieth-century European church history is perhaps the more impressive fact.

37 'The Limitations of William Temple' (1976) p. 38.

38 For a discussion of Niebuhr's influence on Temple, see Alan Suggate (1981) 'William Temple and the Challenge of Reinhold Niebuhr'. I agree with John Kent, though, when he says that Suggate and others overplay the extent to which Temple, under Niebuhr's influence, moved from the optimism of his early theology to a neo-orthodox pessimism about the world in the late 1930s. There was some movement in this direction, as we shall see, but the belief in the possibility of making the world a better place was still strong. See Kent (1992) *William Temple*, pp. 166–7.

39 From 'A Conditional Justification of War', reprinted in *Religious Experience* (1958) pp. 172–3.

40 Suggate, though, simply reports that Temple was heavily criticized for his views (*William Temple and Christian Social Ethics Today* (1987) p. 105).

41 Karl Barth wrote to Bell in the following way: 'Dear Bishop, I think you are too much a British gentleman and thus unable to understand the phenomenon of Hitler.' Hastings, *History* (1987) p. 343.

42 The exception is Joseph Fletcher's *William Temple: Twentieth Century Christian*, publilshed in the United States in 1963. This is a 'portrait' of Temple's thought, with a biographical sketch added at the end. It is an impressive introduction to many aspects of what Temple taught, but it is not a critical study.

43 *William Temple's Philosophy of Religion* (1961).

44 *William Temple's Political Legacy: A Critical Assessment* (1963).

45 'The Limitations of William Temple', *Theology*, January 1976.

46 E. R. Norman, *Church and Society in England 1770-1970* (1976) pp. 282–3. Norman is so critical of Temple that it is hard to see how Temple could have been taken seriously by his contemporaries, let alone become the most influential church leader of his generation. Norman also argues that Temple became more moderate and 'realistic' in his later years (pp. 323–4, 369). But we saw how the campaign which began at Malvern and ended with 'The Church Looks Forward' was, if anything, more radical in its social and political proposals than what he had taught before.

47 Alan Suggate, *William Temple and Christian Social Ethics Today* (1987) e.g. Chapter 11.

48 In 'William Temple', forthcoming *New Dictionary of National Biography*.

49 *William Temple*, (1992) pp. 179–90.

50 In 'William Temple', forthcoming *New Dictionary of National Biography*.

51 *William Temple and His Message* (1946) ed. A. E. Baker, p. 43.

52 *William Temple and His Message* (1946) p. 47.

Bibliography and References

For a longer list of William Temple's writings see Suggate, *William Temple* (1987). For a comprehensive and chronological listing of all his writings see the bibliography in my D.Phil dissertation.

Books by William Temple (in chronological order)

The Faith and Modern Thought. Lectures. London: Macmillan, 1910.

The Nature of Personality. Lectures. London: Macmillan, 1911.

The Kingdom of God. Lectures. London: Macmillan, 1912a.

Repton School Sermons: Studies in the Religion of the Incarnation. London: Macmillan, 1913. *Studies in the Spirit and Truth of Christianity.* Sermons. London: Macmillan, 1914.

Church and Nation. Lectures. London: Macmillan, 1915.

Plato and Christianity. Lectures. London: Macmillan, 1916.

Mens Creatrix: An Essay. London: Macmillan, 1917a.

The Challenge to the Church. Mission account, London 1917b.

Issues of Faith. Lectures, London: Macmillan, 1917c.

Fellowship with God. Sermons. London: Macmillan, 1920.

The Universality of Christ. Lectures. London: SCM Press, 1921a. Reprinted in *About Christ,* London: SCM, 1962.

Life of Bishop Percival, London: Macmillan, 1921b.

Christus Veritas: An Essay. London: Macmillan, 1924.

Christ in His Church. Diocesan charge. London: Macmillan, 1925a.

Christ's Revelation of God. Lectures. London: SCM Press, 1925b. Reprinted in *About Christ,* London: SCM, 1962.

Personal Religion and the Life of Fellowship. London: Longmans Green, 1926.

Essays in Christian Politics and Kindred Subjects. London: Longmans Green, 1927.

Christianity and the State. Lectures. London: Macmillan, 1928.

Christian Faith and Life. Mission addresses. London: SCM, 1931a. Reissued 1963. Page references to this edition. New edition, ed. Susan Howatch, London: Mowbray, 1994.

Thoughts on Some Problems of the Day. Diocesan charge. London: Macmillan, 1931b.

Nature, Man and God. Gifford Lectures. London: Macmillan, 1934.

Basic Convictions. Addresses. London, 1936a.

Christianity in Thought and Practice. Lectures. London: SCM Press, 1936b.

The Church and its Teaching Today. Lectures. New York: Macmillan, 1936c.

The Preacher's Theme Today. Lectures. London: SPCK, 1936d.

Readings in St. John's Gospel. 2 vols. London: Macmillan, 1939–40. Paperback edition 1961 (still in print). Page references to this edition.

Thoughts in War-Time. Sermons and addresses. London: Macmillan, 1940a.

The Hope of a New World. Sermons and addresses. London: SCM Press, 1940b.

Citizen and Churchman. London: Eyre and Spottiswoode, 1941.

Christianity and Social Order. Harmondsworth: Penguin, 1942. New edition London: SCM, 1950. Page references to this edition. New edition: Shepheard-Walwyn and SPCK, 1976, with Foreword by the Rt Hon. Edward Heath and Introduction by Professor R.H. Preston.

The Church Looks Forward. Sermons and addresses. London. Macmillan, 1944.

Religious Experience and Other Essays and Addresses. Posthumous collection. London: James Clarke, 1958.

Some Lambeth Letters, ed. F. S. Temple, Oxford, 1963.

Other writings by William Temple (select list, in chronological order)

The Education of Citizens, Address, London, 1905.

'The Church', 'The Divinity of Christ' and 'Epilogue' in *Foundations. A Statement of Christian Belief in Terms of Modern Thought by Seven Oxford Men.* London: Macmillan, 1912c.

Competition: A Study in Human Motive. London: Macmillan, 1917. Written by a committee of which Temple was a member.

'The Christian Social Movement in the Nineteenth Century', *Christian Social Reformers of the Nineteenth Century,* ed. Hugh Martin, London: SCM, 1927.

'Revelation', *Revelation,* ed. John Baillie and Hugh Martin, London: Faber and Faber, 1937.

'Chairman's Introduction' in *Doctrine in the Church of England, The Report of the Commission on Christian Doctrine Appointed by the Archbishops of Canterbury and York in 1922.* London: SPCK, 1938.

'Christian Faith and the Common Life' in *Christian Faith and the Common Life,* Vol. IV of the Oxford Conference, 1937, On Church, Community and State. London: Allen and Unwin, 1938.

'Introduction' to *Men Without Work. A Report made to the Pilgrim Trust.* Cambridge UP, 1938

'The Chairman's Opening Address' and 'A Review of the Conference' in *Malvern, 1941. The Life of the Church and the Order of Society, Being the Proceedings of the Archbishop of York's Conference.* London: Longmans Green, 1941

'In Time of War' with C. E. Raven in *Is Christ Divided?* Harmondsworth: Penguin, 1943

Other letters and papers

The William Temple papers at Lambeth Palace Library contain many of his unpublished writings and letters, together with copies of nearly all of his published works. A majority of the papers come from his years as Archbishop of Canterbury.

MS 1765 at Lambeth are the letters he wrote to his brother throughout his life, about 700 in all. There are also editorials and articles in *The Challenge, The Pilgrim,* and *The Highway, The Listener.*

Books and dissertations on William Temple (select list)

Carmichael, John D. and Goodwin, Harold S., *William Temple's Political Legacy,* London: A. R. Mowbray, 1963.

Fletcher, Joseph, *William Temple: Twentieth Century Christian,* New York: Seabury, 1963.

Iremonger, F. A., *William Temple, Archbishop of Canterbury: His Life and Letters,* London: Oxford, 1948.

Kent, John, *William Temple: Church, State and Society in Britain 1880–1950,* Cambridge 1992.

Padgett, Jack F., *The Christian Philosophy of William Temple,* The Hague: Martinus Nijhoff, 1974.

Spencer, S. C., *The Decline of Historicism in William Temple's Social Thought,* University of Oxford D.Phil dissertation (in the Bodleian Library, Oxford), 1990.

Suggate, Alan D., *William Temple and Christian Social Ethics Today,* Edinburgh: T and T Clark, 1987.

Thomas, Owen C., *William Temple's Philosophy of Religion,* London: SPCK, 1961.

Other books and articles

Bell, G. K., 'Memoir', in *William Temple and His Message,* ed. A. E. Baker, Harmondsworth: Penguin, 1946.

Bruce, Malcolm, *The Coming of the Welfare State,* London: Batsford, 1961.

Emmet, Dorothy, 'The Philosopher', in F. A. Iremonger, *William Temple* (1948).

Forbes, Duncan, *The Liberal Anglican Idea of History,* Cambridge, 1952.

Hastings, Adrian, *A History of English Christianity 1920–1985,* London: Collins: Fount Paperbacks, 1987.

Hastings, Adrian, 'William Temple' in *The Shaping of Prophecy,* London: Geoffrey Chapman, 1995.

'William Temple', in *The New Dictionary of National Biography,* Oxford, forthcoming.

Hinchliff, Peter, *God and History: Aspects of British Theology 1875–1914,* Oxford: Clarendon, 1992.

Frederick Temple, Archbishop of Canterbury, A Life, Oxford: Clarendon, 1998.

Jenkins, David, 'Christianity, Social Order and the Story of the World', *Theology,* London: SPCK, September 1981.

Lowry, Charles, 'William Temple after Forty Years', *Theology,* January 1985.

Macquarrie, John, 'William Temple: Philosopher, Theologian, Churchman', *The Experiment of Life: Science and Religion,* ed. F. Kenneth Hare, Toronto 1983.

Niebuhr, Reinhold, 'Dr William Temple and His Britain', *The Nation,* New York, 11 November 1944.

Norman, E.R., *Church and Society in England, 1770–1970: A Historical Study,* Oxford: Clarendon, 1976.

Oliver, John, *The Church and Social Order: Social Thought in the Church of England 1918–1939,* London: A. R. Mowbray, 1968.

Peacocke, A.R., 'The New Biology and *Nature, Man and God'*, in *The Experiment of Life: Science and Religion,* ed. F. Kenneth Hare, Toronto 1983.

Preston, Ronald H., 'Thirty-Five Years Later: 1941–1976: William Temple's *Christianity and Social Order'*, in *Explorations in Theology 9,* London: SCM, 1981.

'Middle Axioms in Christian Social Ethics', in *Explorations in Theology 9,* London: SCM, 1981.

'William Temple as a Social Theologian', *Theology,* London: SPCK, September 1981.

Ramsey, A. M., *From Gore to Temple: The Development of Anglican Theology between Lux Mundi and the Second World War,* London: Longmans, 1960.

Rogerson, J. W., 'William Temple as Philosopher and Theologian', *Theology,* London: SPCK, September 1981.

Spencer, Stephen, 'William Temple's *Christianity and Social Order* after Fifty Years', *Theology,* London: SPCK, January/February 1992.

'History and Society in William Temple's Thought', *Studies in Christian Ethics,* Edinburgh: T and T Clark, Vol. 5 No. 2, 1992.

Suggate, Alan D., 'William Temple and the Challenge of Reinhold Niebuhr', *Theology,* London: SPCK, November 1981.

Tawney, R. H., 'William Temple: An Appreciation', *The Highway,* January 1945.

Vidler, A. R., 'The Limitations of William Temple', *Theology,* London: SPCK, January 1976.

Visser't Hooft, Willem Adolf, 'The Genesis of the World Council of Churches', in *A History of the Ecumenical Movement 1517–1948,* ed. Ruth Rouse and Stephen Neill, second ed., Philadelphia: Westminster Press, 1968.

Williams, Canon G. A., *Viewed from the Water Tank: A History of the Diocese of Blackburn,* Preston: Palatine Books, 1993.

Index